Veronica Kelly

Beauty and the Market: Actress Postcards and their Senders in Early Twentieth-Century Australia

A hundred years ago the international craze for picture postcards distributed millions of images of popular stage actresses around the world. The cards were bought, sent,. and collected by many whose contact with live theatre was sometimes minimal. Veronica Kelly's study of some of these cards sent in Australia indicates the increasing reach of theatrical images and celebrity brought about by the distribution mechanisms of industrial mass modernity. The specific social purposes and contexts of the senders are revealed by cross-reading the images themselves with the private messages on the backs, suggesting that, once outside the industrial framing of theatre or the dramatic one of specific roles, the actress operated as a multiply signifying icon within mass culture – with the desires and consumer power of women major factors in the consumption of the glamour actress card. A study of the typical visual rhetoric of these postcards indicates the authorized modes of femininity being constructed by the major postcard publishers whose products were distributed to theatre fans and non-theatregoers alike through the post. Veronica Kelly is working on a project dealing with commercial managements and stars in early twentieth-century Australian theatre. She teaches in the School of English, Media Studies, and Art History at the University of Queensland, is co-editor of *Australasian Drama Studies*, and author of databases and articles dealing with colonial and contemporary Australian theatre history and dramatic criticism. Her books include *The Theatre of Louis Nowra* (1998) and the collection *Our Australian Theatre in the 1990s* (1998).

NEWSPAPERS and press photographs used as secondary sources in theatre history frequently seduce by their sheer artefactual materiality and their memorializing pathos, such that the specific conditions of production and circulation of these literary or visual documents become themselves objects of investigation. Although picture postcards show carefully composed photographs rather than being direct production records, their sometimes brilliant clarity as visual artefacts far surpasses the grainy letterpress production photos published in the early twentieth-century illustrated Australian press.

Picture postcards of performers can also provide valuable if ambiguous evidence about star presence and specific costumes and roles, particularly during the first two decades of last century – the international 'golden age' of the mass-produced picture postcard. While postcards of male performers were also published in volume, the

early twentieth century is predominantly characterized by the mass production of cards of the female performer – the actress.

Such cards held in public collections (or scanned in their thousands on the internet) constitute a vast archive for the study of the social outreach of theatrical imagery and of codings of femininity at a time when commercial theatre was dominated by musical comedy, costume melodrama, variety, and opera. During this period, international steamship and rail communications ensured for performers both intra-national and international mobility through touring. This exposed an increasing number of theatregoers in non-metropolitan countries such as Australia to first-hand contact with major theatre personalities, who were variously recognized, claimed, or acclimatized in more than one country.[1]

Distributed on these same communication systems via international post offices, the performer postcard provided theatre, as a major factor within the cultural processes of early modern globalization, with a mass-industrialized and even more geographically penetrative instrument. Moreover, the mass-produced glamour postcard lies at the intersection of two contemporaneous popular practices – theatregoing itself and the international enthusiasm for postcard collecting – and these activities are interpreted in the particular case of Australian sending and collecting in the decade following Federation (1901–10).

The Potency of Postcards

Rather than being valued purely for their visual possibilities as sources of secondary evidence about theatre practice, both the images themselves and popular usage of mass-produced theatre postcards are the primary objects of this study. To adapt Marjorie Garber's challenge about decoding the transvestite, it is useful to look *at* the glamour postcard rather than looking *through* it.[2] Postally used performer cards are read as evidence for the international social penetration of theatrical imagery by means of modern communication technology. Mass-produced photographic portrait postcards of theatre identities are material documents of a significant social articulation of early modernity: artefacts which derive from theatrical practice, but succeed in extending charismatic presence and signifying potency far beyond their theatre-industrial origins.

Graham Clarke, in his study of portrait photography, declares that:

The photograph displaces, rather than represents, the individual. It codifies the person in relation to other frames of reference and other hierarchies of significance. Thus, more than any other kind of photographic image, the portrait achieves meaning through the context in which it is seen.[3]

Postcard sending and collecting ensured that the informal circulation of the theatrical card freed the cultural image of the performer from the constraints of locality, gender, class, and social capital which limit live theatre attendance, to disperse images of glamour and celebrity into many new reception contexts and across the widest possible territory. This article assesses specifically the actress postcard as a factor in understanding theatre as a social phenomenon in an age of international mass communication practices and institutions – vigorous journalism, accessible photography, cheap publishing techniques, and centralized distribution networks.

The specific nature of the photo of female star performers also requires exploration. Roger Hargreaves writes of the mid-nineteenth century celebrity photographic portrait: 'Social and celebrity images opened the way for the portrait to act up beyond its primary function as a sign of individual identity and to place it at the centre of an increasingly complex set of social relationships. Context became paramount.'[4] The stars themselves, their theatrical fame, the poses, clothes, and modes of iconic beauty they project are historically specific constructions of idealized and glorified femininity transmitted around the world.

The signifiers of beauty, purity, luxury, youth, or elegant charm constructed in the imagery attempt to remove the actress from the problematic moral taint of theatrical inauthenticity or of quotidian labour relations, let alone of that regulated market exchange essential to the functioning of the postcard as commodity. Rather, she is enlisted as an icon of classical bourgeois feminine discourses such as moral idealism and sexual legibility, signified through a flawless and seemingly transparent loveliness which is capable also of projecting a confiding and reassuring emotional accessibility. Paradoxically, just as the actress enters as participant of the age of modern global production and distribution, her image performs as the mass-mechanized mediator of largely pre-modern cultural values, themselves in the process of renovation and re-invention to meet the desires of a mass market.

Today, the advent of the internet has re-established the Edwardian female star as a desirable and collectable commodity. With her fabulous sartorial codes of pearls, lace, furs, feathers, and couture gowns transfigured by radiant lighting, her persona as a

NEW THEATRE QUARTERLY

successor journal to THEATRE QUARTERLY (1971–1981)

VOLUME XX   PART 2   MAY 2004

78

Editors
Clive Barker, Simon Trussler, Maria Shevtsova

*Published in February, May, August, and November by Cambridge University Press, Edinburgh Building,
Shaftesbury Road, Cambridge* CB2 2RU, *England*   ISBN 0-521-60327-7   ISSN 0266-464X

Editorial Enquiries

Oldstairs, Kingsdown, Deal, Kent CT14 8ES, England (simontrussler@btinternet.com)

Unsolicited manuscripts are considered for publication in *New Theatre Quarterly*.
They may be sent to Simon Trussler at the above postal address, but submission
of files as e-mail attachments is now preferred. A guide to the journal's house style
may be downloaded from the NTQ website: www.cambridge.org/journals/ntq

Articles appearing in NTQ are abstracted or indexed in *American Humanities Index,
Arts and Humanities Citation Index, ASCA, America: History and Life* (1991–),
Current Contents, Humanities Index (1988–), *Historical Abstracts* (1991–),
MLA International Bibliography, Annotated Bibliography of English Studies (*ABES*)

goddess of charm and luxury is displayed *en masse* in sites run by public repositories, private enthusiasts of long-ago stars, postcard fans displaying their treasures, commercial card dealers, or auctioneers. A century after their heyday, the beauties of a half-forgotten theatrical tradition are again displayed and marketed internationally, circulating once more via the new global mass-communication medium.[5]

The archive of Australian-located postcards selected for study comprises the hundreds of theatre postcards held in the David Elliott and the Theatre Postcards and Small Photograph Collections in the National Library of Australia in Canberra. These contain photographs created by mostly English or Australian studios which were postally used in the period from 1900 to 1920, and are supplemented by my own collection.[6]

Many of the inscriptions on the NLA cards suggest that they were selected or treasured in albums not only to gratify the recipient with a picture of a favourite, but to complete a collector's set of cards or topics. Fandom, collection, and the ubiquity and convenience of the brief written postcard as a cheap communication medium overlap to embed the theatrical portrait card in a complexity of early twentieth-century everyday practices.

Antecedents and Origins

Picture postcards are a significant early modern mass-cultural phenomenon at present better documented by cartophiles, historians of postal documents, and topographic or social historians than critically investigated for their culturally productive content in the theatrical context.[7] Exceptions are interpretations of theatrical photography as performance evidence, notably Laurence Senelick's studies of the gestural repertoire and erotic codings of the postcard's privately-distributed predecessor, the smaller format *carte-de-visite*.[8] Senelick examines largely European images, whose social uses and sexual codings differ significantly from the kinds of photographs of wholesome dramatic and musical comedy stars thought suitable for widespread postal distribution in the British Empire.

Maria-Elena Buszek writes of how 'nineteenth-century photographic imagery – when created to represent and promote specifically *sexualized* theatrical identities *outside* of the contained space of the theatre – was constructed, circulated, and made visible' (her emphases).[9] Her focus is the *carte-de-visite* pin-up of burlesque actresses in America, and she demonstrates that the circulation of these images 'had the potential to extend far beyond their individual purchase and consumption' to find a prized place – as did the later postcard – 'in the bourgeois collectors' photo albums', alongside the family photographs and the portraits of revered public figures.[10] The transgressive and provocative nature of these *carte-de-visite* images of the theatrical demi-monde differ markedly from those created by the mass incursion of the postal picture card, whose public nature (surveilled by the postal authorities)[11] was to alter the images of femininity chosen by studios and manipulated by the performers themselves into a specific historical manifestation.

Erotic postcards as a genre, including those framed in 'theatrical' settings with models posing as 'actresses', did not of course disappear – in fact they form a huge section of postcard output; but these were largely intended for private collection. The Edwardian female theatrical performer who used commercial publishers of photographic cards to broadcast her image to the world through state-run postal systems produced a different suite of coded signifiers and a less overtly sexualized set of affects to those in the privately-circulated *cartes-de-visite* interpreted by Senelick; yet she was able to benefit from a half-century's tradition of skilful collusion between stars, photographers, card publishers, and theatre publicists.

The modern picture postcard was conceived in Austria or Germany, where, due to the superior colour reproduction techniques available, publishers worldwide sent their cards for manufacture until 1914. The first British postcard appeared in 1870 and was an instant success, despite the Post Office maintaining a monopoly of manufacture which it held until 1894.[12] Among the first uses of postcards were advertisements for commercial firms, especially to advise of dispatch or receipt of parcels. In 1875 New South Wales was the first Australian colony to issue postcards, followed by Queensland in 1880.[13]

The Paris Exhibition of 1889 popularized postcard sending internationally, since visitors to the Eiffel Tower could post them from a special Post Office at the top level: these are seen as the first picture postcards.[14] In 1894 the British postal authorities finally bowed to the pressures of commercial publishers wishing to issue cards to satisfy popular demand. These early 'undivided backs' had an address-only directive on the stamp side and an image on the front which perforce had to be over-written by senders. Such privately printed cards were being produced in all Australian colonies from 1898. In 1902 the Postmaster General in England authorized the divided back postcard with space on the stamp side for both address and message, thus freeing the front to carry an image only and initiating the reign of the picture postcard as art form.[15]

Heyday of the Postcard

The new Commonwealth of Australia did not admit the divided back until January 1905, but the old undivided backs continued in circulation.[16] Whereas in England internal transmission cost a halfpenny, Australians were charged a penny postage for their cards by the colonial post offices, and subsequently by the Commonwealth as it took over national responsibility for the postal service. The cross-class popularity and global penetration of picture cards of any conceivable subject were extraordinary: 'during the years from 1900 to 1910 between one and three million postcards passed through the [British] post daily'.[17] By 1903, 600 million annually were being sent through the English post, and by 1914 it was 880 million.[18]

To meet the varied demands of senders, tourists, and collectors, publishers issued cards on every variety of subject, and theatre cards (frequently classed by collectors as 'glamour') are but a tiny proportion of this enormous output. Many of the theatre-interest cards distributed in their millions were pro-

duced by the major British firms of Valentine, Raphael Tuck, J. Beagles & Co., Philco, Rapid Photo, Aristophot, and Rotary Photographic; and these firms, with the addition of those by Australian studios, account for the bulk of the surviving postcards found in Australia.

Theatre managements saw the advantage of placing on theatre seats free publicity cards showing photographs of current productions. Bland Holt, the Sydney-based Australianizer of Drury Lane melodramas, was a big user of such advertising material, and many production cards can still be found of *The Great Rescue*, *Flood Tide*, *The Welsher*, or *The Bondman*.[19] Australian theatre managers availed themselves of the increased national awareness of their shows (and expensively imported actors) created by the sale of portrait and glamour cards from the major Australian studios such as Rembrandt, Falk, and Talma.[20] These served to build audiences for their specific resident or visiting stars, but overseas postcards sold in bulk also raised enthusiasm for touring celebrities, and for celebrity as such.[21]

Postcards complemented the other visual media such as the illustrated press and foyer publicity portraits. Before the first Australian tour of Oscar Asche and Lily Brayton in 1909, managers Clarke, Meynell, and Gunn displayed photographs of the latter in their Melbourne theatre: 'Some of the loveliest pictures imaginable of the beautiful actress have already been received, and visitors to the Royal, on being afforded a glimpse, have been conquered immediately and become worshippers at her shrine.'[22] Postcards hugely extended the geographical distribution of 'worshippers' at little cost to management, although the personality depicted might now be valued for other reasons than her theatrical artistry or even her fame.

Personality, beauty, desirable fashion, and projected affects of femininity are the qualities that can communicate advantageously on a postcard, and the actress here had to compete within the huge and varied postcard field of glamour photographs of models and of multiple renderings of femininity by postcard artists.

As one consumer choice amidst the huge array of postcard merchandise, Australian studios' postcards sat comfortably beside huge numbers of imported cards depicting performers great and small who never toured there, and whose extra-card theatrical significance may have been of minimal relevance to Australian theatregoers. However, it was not so much the shows as the glamorous idols who provided the attraction for postcard buyers. The actor card might show a performer in identifiable costume, but frequently they are presented detached from specific theatrical context. What is projected through the lens is a fantasy of glamour and distinction, and a free-floating sense of a pleasingly constructed and arresting personality.

A Multiplicity of Identities

In a commodity market, reproduction is advantageously complemented by diversity. The actress 'personality' is usually not a monolithically stable social identity, but rather metamorphically varied through a series of camera-directed scenarios.[23] The theatre critic and journalist Herbert Farjeon recalls how the ubiquitous display of such multiplied images had come to dominate the visual field of English urban life:

[Farjeon] recalled seeing rows and rows of glossy musical comedy beauties in the alluring windows of the stationers. Some of them were smiling to display their dazzling white teeth, some peering coyly over parasols, some swinging on swings, some perching on crescent moons, some revelling in snow, some with their doggies, some punting, some canoeing, some in pyjamas, some in furs.[24]

So too, from the evidence of surviving cards, could the actress postcard be found for sale even in the remotest rural Australian areas, even if their range of styles or quality did not always satisfy the discerning purchaser.

As shown (above right) in the early undivided-back Talma portrait of the Viennese-born singer and Australian favourite Grace Palotta in an oval vignette, with its quotation of classical wreaths and Byzantine gold

Miss Grace Palotta

Talma & Co., Melbourne and Sydney copyright.

background, the visual rhetoric of postcards is frequently affected by manipulation of the plain photo in the process of producing an 'artistic' image.[25] Hieratic iconicity and narrative or mythic visual allusions referring the actress to the bourgeois cultural sphere are often attempted, suggesting that the still-volatile social persona of the female performer is being anchored for a mass market in the safety of the artistically legitimate.

An American studio photographer, Otto Walter Beck, asserted in 1907 that:

Photography enters the field of art guided by the pictorial principle. Photo-portraiture should strive to attain the depths, the tactile quality, the logic and completeness of balance that delight us in masterpieces of drawing or painting in monochrome.[26]

Beck's own technical practice was chemical manipulation of the actual negative, seeking to enhance his subject by the creation of a more suitable compositional background of

over black and white costumes according to caprice rather than any original theatrical design.

Thus, after the colourists of Maud Jeffries in her famous creation of Mercia[29] (left) were through with her virginal white Christian-martyr costume it flourishes in rainbow hues and gold embellishments: the contrast of monochrome printing offers an extensive surface for hand-applied decoration.[30] The tinting, tinselling, and embossing with sequins of the original image to transform it into a kitsch icon for mass distribution usually bear little relation to the structure of the original costume, as crude layers of glued tinsel can overlay the delicacy of lace and ruffles or obscure the elegant cut of a Lucile gown.[31]

'perfectly balanced irregularity',[27] according to the portraiture principles of a Rembrandt or Van Dyck. Actress postcards show the photograph manipulated, situated, and adorned in many ways, both to endow 'artistic' quality and to manufacture useful variations of the original image to suit differing tastes and budgets. As Beck declares, 'the created background in photography is a civilizing agent'.[28] It was also a commercial niche-marketing tool.

More common than Beck's sometimes startling plate-manipulation of commissioned portraits are those later embellishments of glamour postcards where sweatwork hand-colouring freely applies sometimes delicate, sometimes crude and idiosyncratic tinting and decoration on flat rather than plastic principles. Many hand-coloured photographic cards lay irrelevant colour

The hand-tinted and tinselled picture of the musical comedy singer Lily Elsie (opposite page, bottom right) showed some restraint in this tuppence-coloured folk genre.[32] As with many of the star postcard backgrounds, the accessories and background are legibly of the studio, but they still perform Beck's 'civilizing' function by anchoring the feminine in symbolism of luxury, leisure, and pastoral nature. Contrasted with the high formality of the Palotta card's portrait bust contained by its classical oval, Elsie's less formal pose increases access to the body, fashion choices, and fashionable modernity of the actress-star.

The Senders and Receivers

The glamour postcards sent in early Federation Australia display a seeming poignant contrast between the imaginary worlds of luminous loveliness shown in the images and the demotic domesticity of the messages on their backs. These star images are *familiarized* – selected, purchased, inscribed, compared, contrasted, assessed, classified, hunted down, swapped, and collected. The actor image lives on in quotidian domestic contexts: on the mantelpiece, in albums or dusty shoeboxes, treasured in family papers or dispatched to junk shops.

The international icons of glamour served variously as jealously collected possessions and as casual communicative media. They also functioned as iconic symbols of obscure self-enunciation for urban and rural Australian people and working-class families, themselves sometimes far removed from the ideal worlds of non-productive leisure and historical transcendance constructed by these common material objects, which are simultaneously mass-industrialized commodities, miniature artworks, and windows into a nation's dreams.

The cards are inscribed with the variously banal or poignant domestic messages or flirtation codes of their frequently youthful senders and addressees, some of whom resided in remote rural areas where first-hand acquaintance with stellar theatrical glamour would be rare – attained principally through treasured memories of annual theatre visits in the city. The still potent glamour of the cards as social witness to the lives of ordinary people allows some conclusions to be drawn about the cultural positioning and social purposes of the senders and receivers of images from popular theatre. The selection of *postally used* cards immerses one in the social world as well as the cultural sphere of early Federation Australians, whose beloved cards, sent with sometimes private or allusive communicative purposes, now attest to the immediacy and intimacy of daily lives.

Postcards are small scraps of immediacy rescued from death, and their pathos no less than their beauty carries a strong charge. When one compares the handwritten inscriptions with the star images, one can attempt to contextualize the former as creating a kind of feral popular literature, and to read the cards entire as complex cultural documents attesting to the impact of popular international theatre during a newly postcolonial nation's early period of modernity.

An encounter with post-Federation postcards in bulk is to glimpse the social world of working-class and lower-middle class Australians. Their small scale as written documents provided an informal medium for fast communication which risked little loss of cultural face whether for the youthful or the adult poorly-schooled, who 'could still write a short card where a letter's length might have daunted them'.[33]

Specifically, one enters a world of women. The vast majority of posted cards are sent by women, frequently to girlfriends or family members. Male senders are less common, but fathers working hundreds of miles from home greet their children, and jokey brothers indulge the collecting or star-worshipping manias of their sisters. Flirting sweethearts send images or messages fraught with private meanings. The postcard users are often from extended families whose younger members have been dispersed by the labour market across urban and rural areas. Teenage girls frequently work from home as boarding-house domestics in cities or country towns, and the cards record friendships between unmarried young working women and attempts to keep this relationship alive after marriage.

Mothers, whose uncertain skills in literacy suggest childhoods spent before the Australian colonies enacted universal education in the 1870s, labour to keep contact with their children dispersed across the country working on railways, shipping, rural properties, city offices, factories, and shops. On the backs of images of West End idols, greetings are dispatched to relatives, friends, and acquaintances on every birthday and holiday, and the dispatch of parcels and persons is minutely tracked.

In addition to domestic and personal communications, penfriends look for correspondents with whom to exchange cards of mutual interest. Hence, individuals in different areas might now correspond with ease with complete strangers outside the constraints of social and family roles or educational stigma. This was particularly significant for the social lives of women, reconstructed by the postcard's front as consumers, and on its message side as autonomous authors and citizens. 'In some small way the easiness of communication via the postcard . . . has played a part in the long process of [women's] emancipation.'[34] Postcard sending, like literacy and the printing press in Anderson's account, contributed to the building up of a national and international public sphere of informal 'imagined community'.[35]

What postcards *indicate* is multiple: social practices of rural and suburban Australian people; sub-cultures of exchange and desire of the young women who were the major senders and receivers; the important industrial and cultural function of the major Australian photographic studios. The youthfulness of many of the musical comedy stars from George Edwardes's Gaiety and Daly's theatres in London – the international postcard queens Phyllis and Zena Dare, Gabrielle Ray, Billie Burke, Lily Elsie, Gertie Millar, and Marie Studholme[36] – matched that of postcard fans who worked in far less glamorous service positions or industries, including that of postcard production itself.[37]

But, as Ronald Hayman says of the Edwardian matinee idol, deities must never be thought of as working,[38] and they are rarely so framed in the postcard portrait, their labour being occulted while they appear simply 'revelling in snow' or 'playing with their doggies'. In the extant postcard examples theatrical fans seem rarer than card-collecting fans, but the cultures of collectors and that of fans of stars *per se* also overlap with, and extend, the referential fields of readers of theatre journalism and gossip, whether or not these are the same people as actual theatregoers.

But since collecting was taken seriously as an international hobby, and publishing firms catered eagerly to the mass phenomenon by producing cards re-formatting the same image to suit all purses and tastes, correspondents who sent cards hoped to get back cards they liked for their own collection. The early Palotta card (see page 103) sent from Prahran, a suburb of Melbourne, to Miss J. Fraser of up-country Ballarat in 1905, has written on the front: 'Dear Jennie I told you that you could get Grace Palotta my dear I've got 17 actresses Flo'. Another (masculine?) hand adds across the top: 'Sponds are very scarce this week but have managed to get the stamp for this Lyle' (signed twice).[39]

The Theatre Fans

Occasionally cards offer valuable comments from senders about productions they have seen – untapped documentation of the elusive audience testimony so vital to theatre history. One such is a Talma studio card of the American star Maud Jeffries, who toured Australasia from September 1903 to May 1906 co-starring with Julius Knight in Beerbohm Tree productions entrepreneured by J. C. Williamson.[40] She is pictured in her Lady Mary costume for *Monsieur Beaucaire*, but the sender refers to another Jeffries role: 'Isn't she lovely in *The Silver King*?'[41] A sepia Talma study (opposite page) of the American touring star Minnie Tittell Brune in one of her costumes for *Camille*[42] is sent by our earlier acquaintance, Florrie of suburban Melbourne, again to Miss J. Marion Fraser of Ballarat, on 29 March 1905:

'Miss Tittell Brune

Talma & Co., Melbourne and Sydney, copyright.

This is in Camille when you come home you will have to write the whole plot out. How do you like these have you seen any in Ballarat yet. They are very pretty aren't they. When you come back from Horsham I will send the set to Flo.[43]

Here theatregoing as an urban privilege sits comfortably with an extended and informal collectors' mailing circle. It also suggests a *Camille* production conformable with family audiences, and a text which was still enjoying prolonged cultural visibility.

A Talma image of the Australian operatic and musical comedy star Nellie Stewart has the sender 'Rene' write to her addressee, Miss Lachlan of Brookfield, New South Wales, on 14 March 1906: 'Went to Sign of the Cross and had a good time.' Again, the writer refers to another performer and performance: it is

Maud Jeffries whom Rene would have seen in *Sign of the Cross*.[44] A 1911 Sydney sender is more forthcoming about his theatrical experience of *Aladdin*: 'I nearly laughed myself sick.'[45]

The brilliant, short-statured comic George Lauri performed in musical comedies in Australia from 1890 to 1907 in such Edwardes productions as *Florodora, The Orchid, The Girls of Gottenberg*, and *The Dairymaids*.[46] In 1907 a writer in Warrnambool in rural Victoria, comparing present country with well-remembered city delights, sends a card of a costumed Lauri in the musical comedy *The Cingalee* to Miss L. Lange of Mt Gambier, South Australia: 'Enjoyed races, fell in love with W . . . I wish I could see him [Lauri] again. Went for a variety last night nothing in it.'[47] On the front of a Talma monochrome half-length character study of J. C. Williamson's American star the tragedienne Nance O'Neil, posted in Cairns in far north Queensland in 1905 to Miss Minnie Proudfoot in Brisbane, the sender, 'George', writes on the picture side 'Not a bad actress what do you think?'[48] The total of 167 images of Brune from the David Elliott Collection alone posted on the NLA's pictorial catalogue attest to the wide circulation of her image as Williamson's major dramatic star, whose female 'audience' reached beyond theatregoers and Brune's own loyal fans to the wider feminine culture which consumed and exchanged images of loveliness, sophistication, and identity possibilities.

This form of social outreach complements Brune's care in maintaining her epistolary relations with adoring gallery girls, and her genuine popularity as an Australian star appears to have been a largely female creation. The extensive range of her postcard images displays a considerably greater variety of poses and a more extensive repertoire of 'personalities' than those of the actual international star Maud Jeffries, suggesting a far more strategic and inventive use of the post-card medium on Brune's part.

A coloured full-length picture of Brune in evening dress or costume sent from 'KCR' in Sydney to an addressee in the small country community of Richmond is frontally in-scribed: 'I think this girl is lovely KCR'. It is ambiguous whether the 'girl' or the card is the collectable artefact, and the stamp-side inscription tellingly conflates both: 'This is the card I showed you last night. I hope you will like it.'[49]

However, the lady-like rectitude, sexual inviolability, and sweet spirituality which Jeffries projected in her role as the Christian martyr Mercia (page 104, top) communicate well in her photographed image, which thus lends itself to personal appropriation for the affective intentions of postcard senders. A con-temporary saw Jeffries's distinctive quality as 'an air of aloofness . . . a sort of indefinable difference, a half-rapt manner, a suggestion of seeing beyond' – in short 'an ideal repre-sentative of all that is gentle, loving and suf-fering'.[50] And in romantic and allusive mode, 'George' sends Miss Minnie Proudfoot of Brisbane a Falk monochrome seated study of a mature-looking Maud Jeffries, not in her famous flowing robes but in tight-laced and rather unfashionably provincial street clothes and wide feathered hat, with the inscribed inspirational message 'You are like this to me.'[51]

The Collectors

Collectors, then as now, have a keen eye for the market value of postcards as exchange-able commodities as well as symbolic gifts. Too many unequal exchanges provoked pro-test. Liell cites a disgruntled Newcastle male writing in 1906:

Would you try and send me a better class of PC? I never send an actress PC that cost less than 4d. This one cost 6d, but I have a good lot of ex-changes just at present of actresses, good cards that is. That is why I have given up collecting views.[52]

An illegible sender living in Launceston, Tasmania, writes to Miss Dorothy Crisp of Burnie (postmarked 10 April 1905) about a differently processed version of the Talma photo of Stewart discussed above: 'I believe you have this in a better style but even so it might be useful to exchange or would Phyl like it, if she hasn't one.'[53] A Melbourne sender writes to Miss L. McGain in industrial North Melbourne on 10 March 1907 on the back of a soulful Rotary Photo of Millie Legarde: 'Thanks for pretty card hope you like this mine as well as I like yours, there is but a limited supply of proper face studies such as you like but this has a nice expres-sion on sad side'.[54]

Chas. A. Locke also writes to Miss McGain, sending her a classy coloured 'sunk gem' image of Maud Jeffries from London's Philco publishers:

You are right there is no fun in our present method, so we will cry off. I think these two will make us right I owe you one, I have just remem-bered for the one you returned that I sent you that I had already sent. You can send Marie Studholme Gabrielle Ray the Dares and Tittell Brune till Doomes Day.[55]

Charles Locke shows himself completely con-gruent with international taste and fashion, since these English performers (Studholme, Ray, the Dares) account for the vast prepon-derance of surviving cards, while Brune is the most prolific Australian-studio postcard queen. The ubiquity of Studholme's image abroad is no barrier to 'Phyllis', writing in December 1905 from Bundaberg in Queens-land to 'Mr B. L. Martin, Chemist' of Mount Bauple Mill, near the small south-east Queens-land timber town of Tiaro:

Thanks for your lovely PCs I saw all those Xmas PCs in Brisbane and thought that they were very uncommon. Is this the one of Marie you men-tioned. If you have not further use for this you might keep it for me. I have 30 of Marie now.

Phyllis may have been unlikely to retrieve her card, since its theatrically anchored Stud-holme image (opposite page) conforms to the 'popular notion of the [musical comedy] leading lady' described by Cecil Beaton as 'someone with a flashing smile, dimples, a pointed index finger, an hour-glass figure and probably a naughty wink'.[56]

TO WISH YOU A VERY MERRY XMAS

N° X.S.185   ROTARY PHOTO. E.C.

album use. The unposted expensive card and the relatively scarce male actor are likelier to be found in these domestic artefacts.[57] These reflect the taste and interests, and the aesthetic creativity of those who spent patient years hunting up the cards they wanted and arranging them artistically with glosses of hand-drawn decor and theatrical quotations, all pasted-in with newspaper review clippings and lovingly kept theatre programmes.

Other albums are less eclectic than those of fans who collected any image of the adored objects, concentrating instead on high-quality and postally-unused photographs, usually without hand-painting or glitter. These appear to be the property of middle-class people whose aesthetic tastes demanded collecting of quality artistic items for possible investment as well as pleasure. In a world of home-made culture, such albums were talking points for social visits. High-point theatrical experiences could be relived as the participants enthused over or suffered the infliction of material reminders of the shared cultural referential world of theatre, and duly admired the industry and persistence needed to put together so enviable an album.

The enthusiastic accumulation by fans of an unending suite of related images both echoes and subverts the mass mechanical reproduction of the modern celebrity image. Driven by unsatisfiable desire for total possession of the suite of metamorphic constructed identities, the collector cannot rest until she has acquired her idol's every possible variation, thus both driving and appropriating mass consumer culture.

Album-making is a more sociable domestic extension of this. Many postcards in public collections are still found in their original albums. It is here that one encounters the theatrical postcard in the context of other card genres such as greetings, fantasy, topographicals, animals, and the 'saucy' French and German glamour cards bought only for

The Beauties

In June 1907 a nervous twenty-one-year-old Lily Elsie, plucked from provincial touring, created the role of 'Sonya' (Hannah) in George Edwardes's English premiere of Lehar's *The Merry Widow* at Daly's Theatre, London; but here the operetta was produced, house-style, through the performance modes of musical comedy. When Elsie, with the American comedian Joseph Coyne as her Danilo, danced as well as sang the famous waltz, moving in a tight embrace up and down a staircase, 'pandemonium broke out in the theatre'. The reign of European operetta in English-speaking theatre had commenced, and Elsie became overnight both a star and an international celebrity.[58]

Cecil Beaton gives valuable testimony as to the range of affects with which Elsie's many adorers invested her performances: 'She appeared slightly remote, mysterious, lyrical, of an impeccable grace and dignity, but extremely vulnerable and poignant. She tugged at the strings of the heart'.[59] Hyman attests to what contemporaries found as her 'other-worldly, ecstatic quality'; and in the waltz-song performance, where she seemed 'a little strange and remote' in her transfigured ecstacy, he locates the essence of her unique appeal as a performer.[60]

Some of these qualities are apparent in the differently-constructed context of the studio portrait (see page 104, bottom). Cecil Beaton credits the diffused auratic ambience of the Elsie photographs to the older practice of 'conservatory' day-lit studios with their glass ceilings, before sometimes harsher electric lighting was extensively used to dramatize the 'personality' of the subject.[61] To the star-struck Beaton, and doubtless to many international postcard buyers who could never hope to see her in person, Elsie embodied the culturally prized 'English rose' femininity of the Edwardian decade. As we shall see, she was not alone in this.

In a study of the star and the press agent in America, Vincent Landro finds that:

Ethical precepts framed by an older sense of character and glamour were under attack by new conventions that held personal magnetism as the key to advancement. Thus, celebrities were needed whose image combined character and personality, a mix of romantic character and eccentric individualism.[62]

A charismatic or enchanting 'personality' became an increasingly crucial feature of the actor's stock in trade, surpassing in mass appeal his or her mimetic skills of character portrayal. This is certainly apparentt in the Tittell Brune card (page 107), where the presentation of a unique, piquant, and ambiguously sexual 'personality' communicates beyond the framing of her Camille role; the Edna May card (page 112, bottom), discussed below, demonstrates, however, that concepts

of ethically-grounded and transfigured 'romantic glamour' remained viable postcard signifiers in the mass-commodity market. In the actress postcards, the publicity image of the specific performer, whether admired for her performative impact or admired merely for being glamourous and famous, merges neatly with the hegemonic ideal of the culturally validated white woman.

Hargreaves reminds us of the role of portrait photography as contiguous with and implicated in the abiding 'nineteenth-century fascination with social classification and order', and photography's instrumental role in scientific and Darwinian investigations in such taxonomizing disciplines as criminology, anthropology, or studies of pathologized mental states.[63] The actress glamour postcard creates from a narrow range of privileged racial and gender signifiers a utopian discursive realm which seemingly transcends such hierarchical regimes, in which youth, luxury, simplicity, and costumed grace reign, and 'natural' beauty is naturally the possession of young white women.

The glamour postcard indicates how theatrical stars and postcard stars (who could be but were not invariably the same people) presented 'their' image for mass consumption removed from the performative context. Here, the actress ventured into new realms of public consumption and discourse. Tseelon writes of the beautiful woman as assuming increased importance in the

'civilizing process', when active satisfaction became limited and men's desire became regulated, [and] women . . . took on the signification of men's desire as well.[64]

Many commentators attest to the hypnotic cross-gender and cross-age appeal of postcard images. Cecil Beaton states:

My enthusiasm for Lily Elsie started when, at the age of three, I discovered on my mother's bed a tinted picture postcard of this swan-like creature with her jewels dotted with sparkling tinsel. The perfection of her profile sent me into transports.[65]

The juxtaposition of infant, maternal bed, and the location thereon of the transfigured icon of a virtual maternal goddess adorned in auratic brilliance nicely captures complexities and investments in the glamour image variously distributed across age, class, and gender.

Anthony Storr provides a more conventionally Freudian explanation for star worship as an infantile projection into adulthood of an elusive imaginary ideal of perfection driven by ever-unsatisfied desire, and he glosses homosocial attraction as typical of the adolescent need for variously male or female ideal selves, when 'we worship our own sex before we turn to worshipping the other'. Such fantastic longings, he believes, shape culture through the restless power of imagination, and condemn even adults to incomplete satisfaction with the real.[66]

Demographics of Youthful Desire

Popular actress postcards in their volume produce an overwhelming effect of youthful purity and sexual legibility: a catering less for the male gaze than to a demographic of youthful female desire for idealized self-fashioning. A Rotary Photo study of Doris Stocker (above, right) makes comprehensive deployment of the vocabulary of loose but sculptured luxurious hair, studio-floral framing, and the encircling of the face by a curvilinear drape of white muslin, the whole being drenched in a tactile pearly light which dissolves the substance and materiality of the body. With the subject's flesh texture of translucent marble, her smooth modelled face, even teeth, and sweet melancholy gaze, the image performs an exaltation of a specific European class and racial construction of femininity into the realm of the super-human.[67]

Most of the really popular postcard subjects are girlish rather than womanly. Prime examples of the young actress as an icon of white beauty are the much photographed English Dare sisters, Phyllis and Zena. Like many actresses whose cards were widely sought in Australia, the Dares didn't perform there, so their local popularity has to do with desirable beauty rather than with admiration for personally witnessed performing talent.[68] On 9 December 1908, H. Windley (?) writes

to his 'dear old friend' Mr Billy Sutton in Tasmania on a photo by Whitlock and Sons Ltd of a youthful Phyllis Dare (with flowing hair): 'Don't fall in love with this little face.'

Max Beerbohm's impression of the Gaiety's 'Big Eight' showgirls, distinguished from the hard-working chorus and chosen for their height, elegance, and ability to parade high-fashion gowns onstage, was of 'the splendid nonchalance of these queens, all so proud, so fatigued, all seeming to wonder why they were born, and born to be so beautiful.'[69] However, the postcard personae constructed by a Dare or a Stocker retain nothing of the chilly charisma of royalty except its claims to super-human perfection. Rather than affecting a studied disdain, they appear to communicate frankly and ingenuously with the viewer, positioning themselves as daughter, sister, friend, sweetheart – or mirror.

Mixed with these visions of youthful candid femininity in clothed signifiers of luxury, delicacy, and fragility are postcards of older women: now aspirational icons of social and

perhaps most notorious and successful Parisian courtesan, seems to have little troubled either Rotary Photographic in London or the card's addressee, Miss Lou McGain, a worker at the Leviathan Clothing Company, Melbourne.[70]

The photographic subjects are sometimes presented in a prosperous social or domestic role rather than a theatrical one, or in the symbolic vestimentary codes of de Pougy and Stocker. In a Rotary Photo half-length diffused-light study (left), Miss Edna May wearing a delicate costume confection smiles at us with sweet wistful ingenuousness accompanied by her 'doggie'; the latter small beast acting as both a girlish signifier and an important identification bridge for its young purchasers and recipients.[71]

sexual achievement rather than beautiful imaginary friends. Mature glamour can also be detached from the subject's autobiographical or professional circumstances. A card sent in Victoria in 1906 shows the image entire of wealth, beauty, style, and elegance, but the presentation of this contemporary woman is clearly very different from the floaty semi-fantasy dress of Stocker or the pastoral distinction of Elsie. Although they share a vestimentary vocabulary of roses, lacy and feathery textures, lambent pearls, and gauze, and are lit 'conservatory'-style to texturize radiant jewellery and hair and translucent white flesh, there are discernible differences in the signifiers of fashion, class, age, and subtle cultural styles. That its subject is Liane de Pougy, the age's

But study of another monochrome Rotary of May (opposite page, bottom right) shows how her persona can be quite differently constructed by the camera, suggesting that Landro's 'romantic' glamour is a product of pose, lighting, costume, and framing, whereas 'individualism' is inflected by variations within a visual genre. May's face and neck occupy most of the neutral pictorial space, a contrast to the bust or half-length norm for glamour photos.[72] Apart from a severely cropped vestige of a pearled head-dress which might have pointed to a specific theatrical role, the body and jewelled adornments are thrown into high relief, with the face floating free from background cues of mundane social anchoring or the assimilation of the feminine into arcadian nature.

Here, Beck's 'civilizing' background has vanished. Its aura is now displaced by and absorbed into the star's illuminated face, of which her pearls and diamonds signify as materialized intensifications. We seem to be invited into the inner life of this paragon of classical beauty, but the three-quarter face pose with its slightly upward gaze denies us entrance into the consciousness of a desirable enigma. This kind of decontextualized pictorial framing predicts the cinematic language of the close-up, made famous in glamour images of film stars such as Garbo. Clarke says:

For all its literal realism [the portrait photo] denotes, above all, the problematics of identity, and exists within a series of cultural codes which simultaneously hide as they reveal its paradoxical meaning.[73]

Finally, the position of feminine agency and desire in early twentieth-century commercial theatre can be complicated by the evidence of these images. Peter Bailey's account of musical comedy thus links the Edwardian evolution of this form in Britain with the pleasures of modern urban consumerism and increased female presence in retail industries, but also reads in its drilled choruses a reflection of the industrial regulation of the body under mass production. The lavishly consumerist, socially wide-awake and vivacious heroine of this repertoire he finds

a male construction of femininity – reactionary men defining their own New Woman, constructed entirely as an object of the male gaze.[74]

However, it is important also to see that the circulation of the mass-produced postal image projected the musical comedy actress's persona (if not her actual condition as a worker) into distant contexts unreachable by male control. This cultural idealization of the feminine divinity was a willed creation as much of women – whether as theatre audiences, photographic studio labourers, or subjects flexing their new consumer power in the mass market – as of Svengali-like male managers, as women worldwide eagerly adapted and consolidated the image of the theatre star as icon of modern subjectivity.

The production and distribution practices of postcard publishers may have been perfectly acclimatized to international industrial capitalism, yet to the postcard collector every favoured actress – and indeed each of her individual photographic re-inventions of 'romantic glamour' – was discerned and valued as desirably different and unique.

The archive of the glamour postcard of performers sent in Australia before the First World War presents a varied yet unified universe of the technologically transfigured feminine. An actress's youthful legibility as sexual subject, and her ability to meet the camera with the requisite feminine gaze of candour and 'simplicity', allied with a seemingly artless and transparent beauty, are assets to be parleyed into the decontextualized circulation modes of an ideal glamour.

The stage performer's ease in self-construction as character, whether undertaken before the desiring gaze of audience or of camera, endows her with the cultural capital to transform in multiple ways as well as to transfigure her images, giving them an extended range of possible positionings and signifiers. Thus her commercial worth is augmented, while her outreach via popular postcards launches her images into a world where they become the prized possession of the owner-fan. There they attain social and psychological meanings outside the relatively controllable fictional framings of live dramatic performance, and even of her extra-dramatic industrial persona as star.

The performers of the rhetoric of the popular postcard become the holy icons of mass modernity, the blessed virgins of a mechanized secular culture trailing uncanny traces of the glamour of aristocratic and pastoral worlds. The actress is thus literally owned by her immediate public, but owned also by a vast demotic consumership whom she might never encounter in the theatre. Her social roles spill out from the industrial-artistic configuration of commercial theatre, and she becomes a worker in the mass-industrial age's international dream industry.

Notes and References

The postcards of Tittell Brune, Edna May, Grace Palotta, and Doris Stocker are reproduced by kind permission of the National Library of Australia.

1. For information on non-resident stars and companies touring Australia, see Philip Parsons and Victoria Chance, ed., *Companion to Theatre in Australia* (Sydney: Currency/Cambridge University Press, 1995), especially Dennis Carroll, 'American Influences' (p. 46–54); Jim Davis, Elizabeth Perkins, and Tony Mitchell, 'English Influences' (p. 205–9); John West, 'J. C. Williamson's' (p. 299–304).

2. Marjorie Garber, *Vested Interests: Cross-Dressing and Cultural Anxiety* (New York: Harper Perennial, 1993), p. 9. Two publications which examine postcard images and messages together are Tom Phillips, *The Postcard Century: 2000 Cards and Their Messages* (London: Thames and Hudson, 2000); and Pam Liell, *Before the Phone: 100 Years of Postcard Messages* (Strathfield North, NSW: Pam Liell, 1998), the only such investigation in the context of Australian social history.

3. Graham Clarke, *The Portrait in Photography* (London: Reaktion Books, 1992), p. 1.

4. Roger Hargreaves, 'Putting Faces to the Names: Social and Celebrity Portrait Photography', in Peter Hamilton and Roger Hargreaves, *The Beautiful and the Damned: the Creation of Identity in Nineteenth-Century Photography* (Aldershot/London: Lund Humphries/National Portrait Gallery, 2001), p. 51–2.

5. The seductive and intriguing power of the postcard image to interpolate strangers remote in time and space into the world of theatre is being repeated today. Many Golden Age actresses have their dedicated fan sites: Edna May (www.templeresearch.eclipse.co.uk/edna_may); Gabrielle Ray (http://collectorspost.com/Ray.htm); Lily Elsie (http://www.lily-elsie.com/). Billie Burke, Gertie Millar, and the Dare sisters are among many familiar Edwardian postcard icons, the collection of whose cards motivate some website authors to discover and exchange more information about the performers' lives and acting careers.

6. The National Library has led the way in providing online access to its photographic collection and is particularly strong in web posting of theatre material:

http://nla.gov.au/catalogue/pictures. Other major Australian public libraries also provide considerable online access to their picture collections. The State Library of Victoria is found at http://pictures.slv.vic.go.au/. The Pictures and Manuscripts online catalogue of the State Library of New South Wales is at http://www.sl.nsw.gov.au/picman/.

7. Innumerable postcard histories and a copious specialist periodical literature exist to cater for the interests of postal historians, professional and amateur traders and collectors, and social historians of specific themes (e.g., military, topographical, erotic, humorous, shipping, historical, artistic). Brief summaries of the development of the postcard in English-speaking countries can be found in Phillips, and in Tonie and Valmai Holt, *Picture Postcards of the Golden Age: a Collector's Guide* (London: MacGibbon and Kee, 1971). Most include the actress card as part of the myriad thematic and production categories which distinguish the field. In the area of theatre cards, Richard Bonynge's *A Collector's Guide to Theatrical Postcards* (London: Batsford, 1988) reproduces exquisite top-market images of opera, ballet, circus, cinema, music-hall, and musical comedy stars: most such cards are examples of postally unused collector's pieces.

8. See Laurence Senelick, 'Eroticism in Early Theatre Photography', *Theatre History Studies*, XI (1991), p. 1–49; and 'Melodramatic Gesture in Carte-de-Visite Photographs', *Theater*, XVIII, No. 2 (Spring 1987), p. 5–13. Peter Buse problematizes the photograph as performance document in 'Stage Remains: Theatre Criticism and the Photographic Archive', *Journal of Dramatic Criticism*, XII, No. 1 (Fall 1997), p. 77–96. The postcard standard size is 5.5 x 3.5 inches; that of the carte-de-visite 4 x 2.5 inches.

9. Maria-Elena Buszek, 'Representing "Awarishness": Burlesque, Feminist Transgression, and the Nineteenth-Century Pin-up', *The Drama Review*, XLIII, No. 4 (1999), p. 141–62.

10. Buszek, p. 156, 159.

11. Phillips, p. 26–7.

12. Eric J. Evans and Jeffrey Richards, *A Social History of Britain in Postcards 1870–1930* (London: Longman, 1980), p. 3.

13. David Cook, *Picture Postcards in Australia 1898–1920* (Lilydale, Vic: Pioneer Design Studio, 1985), p. 19.

14. Cook, p. 14.

15. Evans and Richards, p. 3, 4.

16. Cook, p. 27.

17. Holt and Holt, p. 43.

18. Evans and Richards, p. 4.

19. Cook, p. 38.

20. Information on the major Australian photographic studios can be found in Jack Cato, *The Story of the Camera in Australia* (Institute of Australian Photography, 1955; 2nd ed., 1977); Barbara Hall and Jenni Mathers, *Australian Women Photographers 1840–1960* (Melbourne: Greenhouse, 1986); Alan Davies, Peter Stanbury, and Con Tanre, *The Mechanical Eye in Australia: Photography 1841–1900* (Melbourne: Oxford University Press, 1985); and Gael Newton, Helen Ellis, and Chris Long, *Shades of Light: Photography and Australia 1839–1988* (Sydney; Canberra: William Collins/Australian National Library, 1988).

21. Herbert Farjeon, writing in the *Morning Leader* in 1945, recalls: 'The picture postcard boom was a godsend to the box office when leading musical comedy actresses went on tour. Whenever Zena Dare toured in Seymour Hicks's shows shoals of admirers of her picture post-

cards came to the theatre to see her.' Cited by Alan Hyman, *The Gaiety Years* (London: Cassell, 1975), p. 136. The same could be said for Australian touring idols such as Minnie Tittell Brune and Lily Brayton.

22. *Table Talk* (Melbourne), 18 March 1909, p. 22.

23. A contrast to the cards studied here are those of the much-travelled contralto Dame Clara Butt, usually found photographed half- or full-length and wearing street or evening dress, and projecting a formidable social authority. These images anchor her in a context of bourgeois respectability as 'Mrs Kennerly Rumford', rather than in the fantasy world of radiant light, tinsel, vestimentary transparency, and playfully personalized emotional engagement with the viewer typical of the musical comedy actress card.

24. Hyman, p. 136.

25. David Elliott Collection, NLA, Q15, Box 2, PIC/7350 (online catalogue item nla.pic-an23752565).

26. Otto Walter Beck, *Art Principles in Portrait Photography: Composition, the Treatment of Backgrounds, and the Processes Involved in Manipulating the Plate* (New York: Becker and Taylor, 1907; rpt. New York: Arno Press, 1973), p. 15.

27. Beck, p. 69.

28. Ibid., p. 167.

29. Jeffries created the role of Mercia for *The Sign of the Cross*, which premiered in St Louis on 27 March 1895 and opened in London on 4 January 1896 for 435 performances, becoming thereafter a world success. Written by the actor-manager Wilson Barrett to counter the 'unwholesome tendencies' of the contemporary Ibsenite problem play and to feature 'a woman with a future instead of a past', the play's end has the heroine and her would-be lover Marcus Superbus walking hand-in-hand towards the arena lions. See James Thomas, *The Art of the Actor-Manager: Wilson Barrett and the Victorian Theatre* (Ann Arbor: UMI Research Press, 1984), p. 129; David Mayer and Katherine Preston, ed., *Playing Out the Empire: 'Ben Hur' and Other Toga Plays and Films, 1883–1908: a Critical Anthology* (Oxford: Oxford University Press, 1994). Jeffries, born in Memphis, USA, toured extensively with Barrett in Canada and the USA in Shakespeare and in Barrett's own plays. She performed in *Twelfth Night* with Beerbohm Tree and Lily Brayton, and worked in other English theatres before her Australian tour in 1903–1906; thereupon, having meantime married a New South Wales squatter, she retired from the stage.

30. Author's collection.

31. It should be pointed out that many hand-coloured postcards, and many of the tinselled ones, are exquisite artefacts: other adornment practices were the embossed raising of the card surface, the use of soft tactile paper, and the adhesion of fabrics or feathers. The Canadian-born *couturière* 'Lucile' (Lady Lucy Duff Gordon), the first English fashion designer to challenge the dominance of Paris fashion houses, united fashion and theatre by designing both high-fashion luxury gowns and luxury costumes for the West End musical comedy stage. She was less a dressmaker than what today would be called an image consultant, claiming that she designed Lily Elsie's 'personality', walk, and gestures for her *Merry Widow* role. See Lady Duff Gordon, *Discretions and Indiscretions* (London: Jarrolds, 1932), p. 102. An account of fashion's mutual relations with theatre in this period can be found in Joel H. Kaplan and Sheila Stowell, *Theatre and Fashion: Oscar Wilde to the Suffragettes* (Cambridge: Cambridge University Press, 1994).

32. Author's collection.

33. Liell, 'Introduction', n.p.

34. Phillips, p. 18.

35. Benedict Anderson, *Imagined Communities: Reflections on the Origins and Spread of Nationalism* (London: Verso, 1983). The communication infrastructures provided by the new Australian Federal and State governments are relevant here: with three posts daily in the immediate post-Federation period, a morning message could cross a city and the reply return in time to arrange a social occasion for that evening: the informality of email is matched by the immediacy of the phone call.

36. For an extensive account of the evolution of English and American musical comedy, and the central role of the Gaiety manager George Edwardes and the female leads whom he made world-famous stars and/or peeresses, see Kurt Ganzl, *The British Musical Theatre Volume 1: 1865–1914* (London: Macmillan 1986).

37. Women worked in the mass-manufacture of photographs and of postcards; 'thousands of women' were employed in the production processes of the early Australian studios (Newton *et al.*, p. 77).

38. Ronald Hayman, 'The Last Idols?' in Anthony Curtis, ed., *The Rise and Fall of the Matinee Idol: Past Deities of Stage and Screen, Their Roles, Their Magic, and Their Worshippers* (London: Weidenfeld and Nicholson, 1974), p. 183.

39. 'Sponds' means 'spondulicks' or money. Palotta toured Australia extensively for various managements between 1895 and 1915, arriving first with the Williamson and Musgrove London Gaiety companies which introduced to Australasia the new English genre of musical comedy, with *In Town*, *A Gaiety Girl*, and *The Shop Girl*. Her biggest success was in Leslie Stuart's *Florodora* in 1900. See John West, 'Gaiety Theatre Companies'; and Alwyn Capern, 'Grace Palotta', in Parsons and Chance, p. 240–1, 424.

40. This season commenced with Henri Bataille and Michael Morton's adaption of Tolstoy's *Resurrection*, and included also from the Tree repertoire Hall Caine's *The Eternal City* and David Belasco's *The Darling of the Gods. Monsieur Beaucaire* by Booth Tarkington adapted by E. G. Sutherland was also played along with other costume romances and a popular revival of Knight's hit *The Sign of the Cross*.

41. Picture Collection, Performing Arts Museum, Melbourne. The Knight–Jeffries *Silver King* premiered at Her Majesty's, Melbourne on 21 May 1904. Jeffries had played the role of Nelly Denver in England and the USA; it was Knight's first Wilfrid Denver; see advertisement, *The Age* (Melbourne), 25 May 1904, p. 12. During this season local studio portraits and production photos appear in illustrated papers, and postcards are repeatedly advertised as being on sale at the theatre: 'MAUD JEFFRIES – JULIUS KNIGHT – PICTORIAL POST CARDS (Autographed) on Sale at Her Majesty's: 12 for 6d' (*The Age*, 25 April 1904, p. 10).

42. At the age of twenty-one the unknown American 'emotional actress' Minnie Tittell Brune (*c.* 1883–?) became a phenomenal Australian favourite. Her *Camille* premiered on 11 February 1905 at the Princess's Theatre, Melbourne, and the closeness to the postal date of Florrie's card suggests that the production's fame was current in the city and that Florrie may even have seen it. Brune toured for J. C. Williamson 1904–1907 and again in 1909, starring in such tragic pieces as *L'Aiglon*, *Theodora*, *Romeo and Juliet*, *Camille*, *La Tosca*, and *Leah Kleschna*; also the comedies and modern plays *Sunday*, *The Second Mrs Tanqueray*, *Merely Mary Ann*,

Dorothy Vernon, *Girl of the Golden West*, and *Diana of Dobsons*. In 1906 an Australian vehicle, *Parsifal; or, The Redemption of Kundry*, was written to provide an original showcasing of her girlish but ambiguously provocative sexuality, and in 1908 she was also Australia's first-ever Peter Pan. See Veronica Kelly, 'J. C. Williamson Produces *Parsifal: or, The Redemption of Kundry*: Wagnerism, Religion, and Sexuality', *Theatre History Studies*, XV (1995), p. 161–81.

43. Theatre Postcards and Small Photographs, including John Dease Collection and Mrs James Collection, NLA, Q15 Box 1, PIC/7347. Online image: nla.pic. an23752227.

44. Author's collection. The writer and actor Wilson Barrett's Roman Empire religious melodrama *The Sign of the Cross* premiered in Australia in May 1897, starring Julius Knight and Ada Farrar, and was revived by popular demand for the Knight–Jeffries tour, when the latter recreated her original role of Mercia.

45. Liell, p. 19.

46. See Alwyn Capern, 'George Lauri', in Parsons and Chance, p. 323.

47. David Elliott Theatrical Postcard Coll., NLA, Picture Album 998/358–490.

48. Author's collection. In 1900 O'Neil was the first to perform the role of Hedda Gabler in Australia.

49. Author's collection.

50. Boyle Lawrence, ed., *Celebrities of the Stage* (London: Newnes, n.d.), p. 35.

51. Both cards in author's collection. A copy of the Jeffries image is held at PIC/6492, NLA (nla.pic-an 23217638).

52. Liell, p. 25. The sender's exemplary sixpenny card is a 'large-letter' type where flowers, views, and a motley array of actresses peep from inside a large capital letter, in this case 'G'.

53. Author's collection.

54. David Elliott Coll., NLA, Q15 Box 1, PIC/7549 (nla.pic-an23751806),

55. David Elliott Coll., NLA, Q15 Box 1.

56. Author's Collection. Cecil Beaton, 'Lovely Lily Elsie', in Curtis, ed., p. 7.

57. These include, e.g., NLA Album 386 (1880–1900), Album 175, and Album 646. The first and last of these seem assembled by devoted Brune fans who have traced every image of their idol and requested signed cards. Album 386 is the work of a theatre fan and idolater who arranged the cards in graceful sprays surrounded by Shakespeare quotations (' She is a most exquisite lady') , and pasted-in theatre reviews. Friends have signed comments at the end of the album on its artistic worth and social interest.

58. Hyman, p. 154. There are many memorial accounts of the circumstances of this famous premiere; see e.g. Hyman, p. 146–56; Ursula Bloom, *Curtain Call for the Guv'nor: a Biography of George Edwardes* (London: Hutchinson, 1954), p. 209–18.

59. Beaton, 'Lovely Lily Elsie', p. 7.

60. Hyman, p. 177, 155.

61. Beaton, 'Lovely Lily Elsie', p. 11.

62. Vincent Landro, 'Faking It: the Press Agent and Celebrity Illusion in Early Twentieth-Century American Theatre', *Theatre History Studies* (June 2002), p. 95–115.

63. Hargreaves, p. 5.

64. Efrat Tseelon, *The Masque of Femininity* (London: Sage, 1995), p. 24.

65. Beaton, 'Lovely Lily Elsie', p. 13.

66. Anthony Storr, 'The Loved Ones', in Curtis, p. 191, 193.

67. David Elliott Coll., NLA, Q15, PIC/7351 (nla.pic-an23753519)

68. A monochrome Philco, 'Names and Their Meanings' (Series 6115E), in the author's collection, sent between two females, depicts the youthful Phyllis Dare in soft white shawl and piled-up hairstyle, the photograph vignetted by studio roses and ivy. The name 'Phyllis' is complemented by the caption 'Simplicity'. Here the ideology laboured at in this genre of actress study breaks through into explicit enunciation, while the actress constructs by her gaze and costume its hegemonic form of morally legible feminine sexuality – one which has legitimized social presence and value yet is without threat to herself or her viewer.

69. Hyman, p. 71–2.

70. Theatre Postcards and Small Photographs Col., NLA, Q15 Box 1, Item 7550 (nla.pic-an23751763-0-v1).

71. Author's collection. Edna May Pettie (1878– 1948) was eighteen when in 1897 she was advanced from the chorus to take the female lead in Charles Morton and Gustave Kerker's *The Belle of New York* at George Lederer's Casino Theatre, New York. The Australian impresario George Musgrove, then lessee and manager of the Shaftesbury Theatre, took the gamble of importing the entire production to London in 1898, where it became an overnight success, '[shaking] the staid English out of their antediluvian calm' and made them applaud like an Australian audience, according to Musgrove's partner Nellie Stewart in *My Life's Story* (Sydney: John Sands, 1923), p. 115–16. *Belle* was the first internationally famous American musical comedy, and its young star Edna May became the toast of London and an international property, managed by Charles Frohman and George Edwardes. Stewart found May 'beautiful and sweet as a spring morning' (p. 115), while the *Referee* considered that 'Nobody . . . was ever so innocent as Edna May looks' (quoted in Ganzl, p. 925). After performing continuously on the West End and Broadway, she retired from the stage in 1907 to become Mrs Oscar Lewisohn.

72. Theatre Postcards and Small Photographs Coll., NLA, Q15 Box 2, PIC/7348 (nla.pic-an23752533).

73. Clarke, p. 4.

74. Peter Bailey, 'Musical Comedy and the Rhetoric of the Girl, 1892–1914', *Popular Culture and Performance in the Victorian City* (Cambridge: Cambridge University Press, 1998), p. 175–93.

Janet Lansdale

Ancestral and Authorial Voices in Lloyd Newson and DV8's 'Strange Fish'

Lloyd Newson has worked in Europe for some twenty-three years with DV8 Physical Theatre, creating powerful socio-political pieces which address sexuality and interpersonal relationships. These works are generally created with performers through workshop processes and collaboratively with composers. London's experimental dance and theatre scenes in the 1980s and early 1990s provided a challenging context for Lloyd Newson's early creative endeavours. Here, Janet Lansdale takes one work, *Strange Fish*, as the locus of her discussion on narrative positions in relation to dominant forms of modern dance and issues of sexuality, homophobia, and politics within physical theatre. She conceptualizes and contextualizes 'voices' as 'authorial' and 'ancestral', and traces their manifestation in readings of the work. Complementary and sometimes competing voices from author, text, reader, and cultural history are articulated through a range of intertextual perspectives. This is the second in a series of articles on this work.[1] Janet Lansdale is Distinguished Professor in Dance Studies at the University of Surrey, where she was Head of Department, and later Head of the School of Performing Arts. She is the author and editor of four books on dance theory, history, and analysis, the most recent being *Dancing Texts: Intertextuality in Interpretation* (1999).

FIRST, I shall set the scene by sketching very briefly notions relating to narrative that are particularly relevant to *Strange Fish*. That the creator and performers (Lloyd Newson and collaborators in the company DV8) have a narrative position is perhaps as obvious as the narrative position of the writer of this article. But there are also many other authorial and ancestral dances and sonorities that set the context. These are the dancescapes and soundscapes of the last five centuries in Christianized countries.[2]

There are the narratives that we inherit and absorb often without directly recognizing them, from the body of scholarly writing in dance and physical theatre. They are evident in discourses found in a range of publications and images, from popular journalism to books and journals. The voices that are audible in *Strange Fish*, a physical theatre work first shown in 1992 and subsequently reworked for video in 1994, are many and varied. Newson's intentions and practices did not coincide happily with many of the existing dance voices – primarily those of abstract modern dance inherited from the US –

and I articulate these positions in the first part of the paper.

I make use in particular of the idea of 'ancestral scholarly narratives' of intertextual theory to construct an open-ended argument tracing some of the layers of analysis the work invites. *Strange Fish*, I argue, invites the reader to produce multiple traces, through the process of setting in play different texts and intertexts. As the reader adopts different positions, so different texts come into focus. Expressed in another way, different 'voices' sing at different moments. In addition to the usefulness of the idea of 'voice' in tracing intertextual threads, the presence of actual and ethereal voices in *Strange Fish* give this theme particular poignancy.[3]

Pre-Birth Voices of Newson and DV8

Lloyd Newson's ancestral voices are found in the white, American/Australian/European nexus of 1970s youth culture, in theatre dance, and in popular physical arts. He was born in 1957 in Australia and, while studying psychology at Melbourne University at both undergraduate and postgraduate levels, he danced in the Modern Dance Ensemble, an amateur group with release and improvisation interests. Newson came to the UK in 1980, studied briefly at the London School of Contemporary Dance, and joined Extemporary Dance Theatre (EDT) in 1981, producing an early company piece alongside another newly emerging (and equally controversial) choreographer, Michael Clark.[4] At that time, Emilyn Claid, the Director of EDT, was also commissioning works from other new dance choreographers such as Jackie Lansley, for *Speaking Part* (1981), and Fergus Early, for *Napoli* (1982). While Newson might have been impatient to move on, he was already in the only mainstream company in the UK with experimental ambitions, which he acknowledges in interview with Andy Solway.[5]

Newson started his own group, DV8 (deviate) Physical Theatre in 1986, as an independent collective. Among its stated aims was 'to re-invest meaning in dance', clearly implying that modern dance had lost its way and no longer dealt with meaning. Newson's extension of early twentieth-century Expressionist theatre and dance movements is peculiarly European in character, in its focus on the intensity of emotion and on the use of images, words, and movement, separately and together, treating personal, social, and politically intense subject matter. This trend reverberated further than physical theatre to classical ballet and modern dance, where it is embodied in expressionistic treatments of traditional subject matter in these forms, too, although not to the same extent and in very different movement vocabularies.[6]

Dancing Voices of the 1980s

By the 1980s and 1990s there existed competing, even mutually exclusive, positions on what was perceived to be 'new' and of value in the contemporary dance scene. I articulate these voices through a comparison of critical views to reveal shifting genre and style boundaries. A useful site is found in annual festivals such as those of Dance Umbrella and Spring Loaded (both London events), which present a large amount of new work.

The group of articles referred to below reflect a ten-year shift across the British dance scene.

Fiona Burnside identifies what she calls 'original' and 'mature' voices in 1980s–1990s British 'contemporary dance' in the work of Richard Alston, Laurie Booth, Rosemary Butcher, and Siobhan Davies. Although recognizing that they do not together make a 'united school of thought based on a common philosophy', she suggests that they none the less share a 'cultural and social heritage which has influenced their absorption and transformation of contemporary dance'.[7] The qualities and concerns seen in the 'integration of the elements of production' separates these collaborations from the 'jarring juxtapositions of other European work'. In the same breath, she remarks on the conspicuous absence of the kind of 'dramatic narrative . . . emotional expression, and sexual relations . . . shock tactics . . . political ideology' credited to Lloyd Newson.

Burnside sketches the parameters of what might be termed a distinct style, which she likens to 'the exposition, modulation, and recapitulation of a musical score' rather than to 'Aristotelian cathartic theatre'. To support this argument she states that a degree of dedication 'to exploring the formal properties of the dance medium' is obvious where 'intellectual pleasure in . . . patterning and a sensual enjoyment of the smooth textures of the movement and the colour range' are most evident. This was hardly a productive starting place for Lloyd Newson.

An 'elegant and reticent aesthetic', but one based on a wider range of themes and moods, characterizes Siobhan Davies's 'bodies in motion', building a 'corporate psyche' rather than individual personalities. A 'wider world is invoked' and a 'larger canvas of human suffering' than (she suggests) Rosemary Butcher ever creates.[8] Again, this is some distance in stylistic concerns from Lloyd Newson's apparent interests, despite shared reference to an external world. Laurie Booth, Burnside argues, contrasts most obviously with the others and, in deriving his movement in part from martial arts, physical theatre, and contact improvisation, sows the seeds of shared concerns with Newson.

Booth, however, unlike Newson, elicits response from 'the physical embodiment of the work and not through emotional engagement.

Roughcut, Richard Alston's work discussed by Burnside, is untypical, although sharing with his other works 'technically demanding, physical exploration' which requires 'swift, clean execution and vital energy'. She argues that his work has a greater range of reference to narrative elements, representation, and literary themes than any of the other three choreographers in this group.[9] This, too, is hardly comfortable artistic company for Lloyd Newson.

Constanti provides something of a counterbalance to Burnside by considering very different types of work in the 1987 Spring Loaded festival at The Place which, she argues, revealed two opposing schools of thought, 'dance which appears to be based (naively?) on 'gratuitous pyrotechnics . . . [and] the retaliatory movement stemming from a vigorous personal/social/political stance'.[10]

She refers to Images and La Bouche's work in terms of 'gratuitous pyrotechnics' and, separately, to the personal stance of Emilyn Claid, Liz Aggiss, and DV8. Reluctance to let 'tragedy become beautiful' is shared by this second group, which she describes as embodying 'hard hitting and compulsive' realism and physical/emotional risk-taking – a more obvious connection for Lloyd Newson.

Unexpected shifts on the borderlines between 'witty nonsense' and 'vicious parody' make Lea Anderson's work for the Cholmondeleys clearly distinctive even while she shares some of these features. Her work is individual in its 'rich, abstract vocabulary, the secret cues and whispers are built into a weird, hermeneutic grid of movement, magically sustained by the infernal animation of Drostan Madden's music – a blend of *Velvet Underground*, saxophone . . . and accordion'.[11]

In 1996, nearly ten years later, Jann Parry reflects on the diversity within 'new dance' and particularly in cutting-edge work. She identifies a distinctive concern with constructing narrative and a trend towards spectacle and theatre, a more comfortable environment in which Lloyd Newson plays an important part.[12] Parry constructs a number of categories and spans a huge field; firstly, ballet-derived work as in the newly re-formed Ballet Rambert under Christopher Bruce; secondly, two individuals, Alston and Davies, as the creators of modernist, developed versions of established contemporary dance techniques.

Emerging more clearly in her account are performers working with a highly physical approach – sometimes called Eurocrash companies. Anne Teresa De Keersmaeker, Wim Vandekeybus, and Claude Brumachon are placed here, but so, too, are circus-trained groups. She links dancers who use martial arts, including Laurie Booth and Russell Maliphant, as a fourth stream; while a fifth category, of English Eccentrics, includes 'an assortment of choreographers whose work is highly idiosyncratic'. Here Parry refers to vastly different individuals from Javier de Frutos to Julyen Hamilton, including Wayne McGregor, Matthew Hawkins, Yolande Snaith, Lea Anderson, Liz Aggiss, and Jonathan Burrows. 'Mature performers', whom she groups separately, include Misha Baryshnikov and Fergus Early.

To this amorphous group of categories, she adds 'club and rave culture' (Bunty Matthias), 'text-based work' (Nigel Charnock, V-Tol, and Second Stride), 'cross-cultural/intercultural groups' (Vivarta festivals and Shobana Jeyasingh, Peter Badejo), and finally 'new technology dance' (Mark Baldwin).[13] So the dance world in which Newson worked between 1987 and the end of the 1990s offered some compatible voices and a number of clearly incompatible ones.

A Post-Expressionist Narrative

Newson's relationship to the ancestral voices of the expressionist tradition is revealed in his deep concern with the legibility of dance. His work relies on his collaborators to 'reveal something of their inner selves', to the degree that the performer may feel 'totally exposed and vulnerable'.[14] He challenges the modernist idea of the construction of emotional archetypes, aligning himself with postmodernist works in the 1980s which, more typically, draw on autobiography without reserve rather than abstracting from it.[15]

Among the traces of expressionism that may not be obviously relevant is Newson's inheritance of an actual European expressionist dance movement in his native Australia. This tradition owed its origins to Gertrud Bodenwieser's move from Austria in 1938, in the face of difficult political circumstances, to the Southern Hemisphere, where she took Ausdruckstanz.[16] I do not suggest a direct 'influence' but rather an atmosphere, a culture, of which he was a part and whose voices are still heard. Newson's work is much more than re-articulations of 1930s expressionistic ideas, even though those voices are audible. He has expressed interest in constructing stories that might serve either stage or film and which function through metaphor and allegory.[17] Far from taking existing stories as the *basis* of his work, he states that he 'start[s] from an idea and then look[s] for texts with which I can have a *dialogue*' (my italics). He also refers to starting from an image – a clue that seems to inform *Strange Fish* in its use of the Cross, in the communion wine, in the presence of candles, and in the lighting choices that evoke religious moods.[18]

Newson reworks ideas within a topical 1990s political agenda using many media, including words. In this sense he flouts the highly valued integrity of expressionist dance – its central concern being for expression through movement alone. Autobiographical fragments published in interviews with Andy Solway, Jann Parry, and Nadine Meisner reveal Newson's view that what dance can do best is deal with 'a very personal investigation' rather than 'social and political themes on a larger theoretical level'.[19] These personal investigations often concern the individual's place in society and the exclusion of individuals from particular societies.

Two threads can be woven here into the argument. When challenged by a feminist accusation of sexism, he takes up the victim position, saying 'everybody in my pieces were [sic] victims . . . we're using the work to explore issues which caused us unhappiness, brought about by our own abilities – as gay men, women – to play underdogs and accept

that'.[20] But in recent political argument, and in feminist and post-colonial theory, the notion of difference would be more important than the shared one of victimhood.

The experience of homophobia is different for men and women, and for different age groups; victimhood is different for varied shapes and sizes of people, and for black and white people. Most importantly, the experience of men and women is different, even in contemporary culture. While these voices compete, Newson seems to essentialize experience, a position which is entirely consistent with his expressionist and social-realist views on art, but one which fails to address difference. Newson even constructs a personal narrative for the dancers based on psychological analysis and a concern with spirituality (a theatre of alienation, perhaps), saying: 'Wendy has lost faith, she's lost friendship, she's lost one of the people she wants as a friend, Nigel, largely through her own actions, and she has isolated herself. In her desperate need for friendship, she has actually alienated herself to the point that she has lost all sense of belief and faith.'[21]

The Voices of Collaborators

The dancers' individuality and personal commitment are given a voice through improvisational working methods. Parry refers to a three-and-a-half-month period spent improvising and shaping material to create *Strange Fish* collectively. Newson's collaborators range widely in experience, age, and physique, but each is capable of meeting the challenge of developing movement that is distinctively his/her own, yet appropriate to the theme.[22]

The individuality of modernism is the vocal thread here. Newson makes particular reference to Diana Payne-Myers's 'fragility and her age',[23] but social voices also enter in the nature of the roles taken by Diana Payne-Myers. She is over sixty years old, and she is sometimes abused, exposed unmercifully – perhaps recalling problems the elderly may face in some circumstances. This theatre of cruelty is revealed in a stage scene not used in the video of *Strange Fish* and in another work, *Enter Achilles* (1995).

STRANGE FISH: an outline

	Duration	Mins	Summary Title
1	00.00–03.17	3.17	Church Scene 1. Religious observance
2	03.17–04.42	1.25	Corridor Scene 1. Interrupted conversations
3	04.04–10.52	6.10	Bar Scene 1. Intimidation, competition, and co-operation
4	10.52–15.30	4.38	Bar Scene 2. Sexual play, two against one (female/male)
5	15.30–19.08	3.38	Corridor Scene 2. Dissolving the self, male-female duet
6	19.08–23.35	4.27	Bar Scene 3. The party, the isolate, and the group
7	23.35–27.43	4.08	Room Scene 1. On being alone and together
8	27.43–30.00	2.17	Corridor Scene 3. Intimacy interrupted
9	30.00–39.00	9.30	Room Scene 2. Pointless sex and its aftermath
10	39.30–45.03	6.00	Corridor Scene 4. Brief tenderness turns to violence
11	45.30–49.15	3.45	Room Scene 3. Baptism and absolution
12	49.15–54.20	5.05	Church Scene 2. The desecration of the Cross

In interview, Newson emphasizes the importance of the collaborative process. Yet the performers' openness to improvising and to taking responsibility, which he cherishes, has to be balanced against his statement that 'ultimately I do make the decisions, set exercises and edit material'.[24] In the end, the 'authorial voices' are reduced, or at least focused, through Newson. However, the performers are not the only collaborators, since powerful musical voices intervene.

Ancestral Musical Voices

The performer/singer Melanie Pappenheim and the composer Jocelyn Pook shared an interest in semi-staged and movement-rich performance long before their collaboration in *Strange Fish*. Their focus had often been on palindromic verbal and musical structures and on polyrhythmic constructions, of which an earlier composition, *A Man, a Plan, a Canal, Panama* is an example. Like Pappenheim, Pook is eclectic in her interests and in the range of her work. Both enjoy moving across genres to bring elements of different histories into relationship.[25]

Among the nostalgic forms relevant to the music, as well as to the action, of *Strange Fish* is the Lament, a historically varied musical and poetic form inspired by rites for the dead or ritual leave-taking (bridal laments). This ceremonial form balances the involuntary cry of grief (the 'planctus') and the deliberate framing of a message (the 'discourse'), representing crisis and order respectively.[26] In many cultures lamenting is a task entrusted to women, as it is here. The obsessional qualities of the lament are found also in Monteverdi and Purcell, where music becomes a site of excess, a deviation that must be overcome. There is an obvious link to the nostalgic longing for Christ found in *Strange Fish* and in the compassion for human suffering that Melanie Pappenheim's 'lament' evokes. The understanding of this lament is complicated by the earlier role adopted by this performer as a female Christ-figure. In the lament, she becomes Mary, Mother of God and Intercessor for us all.

Even more obvious is the use of plainsong as a melodic thread through *Strange Fish*, structuring the musical ideas of Scenes 1, 5, 9, 11 and 12 (see the outline structure, above). The improvisatory vocalizing, typical of plainsong, is inescapably associated with woman, although this contradicts historical traces of the male-only plainsong practice of earlier centuries. Jocelyn Pook and Melanie Pappenheim's music reflects plainsong and lament quite strongly, despite their late-twentieth-century position; and the music is a patchwork of improvised elements. They readily acknowledge their starting points in the requiem mass, but worked without recognizable language, and with an awareness of both folk and religious texts, as well as theatrical interests. Their use of prose rhythm provides another direct link to the plainsong period.

Contemporary Traces of Ancient Greece

Newson is particularly indebted to the well-known myth of Heracles. It is the siren figure and men's inability to resist the sensuality of women which is traced from these sources. But there is more than one version of the siren stories, and an interesting ambiguity appears in the final scene where Wendy Houstoun, having climbed the cross to reach Melanie Pappenheim, pours the holy wine down her throat and then appears to 'kiss' her – resoundingly, some critics thought. However, there is also evidence of another trace of the myth, which talks of sucking the breath from the dying body. To see *Strange Fish* as based in several myths and worked through as a 'rite', may help to explain its effectiveness and power. Rather than being dependent on external violence, it operates persuasively through its own effects, generating laughter, seducing the emotions, provoking the reconsideration of ideas, swallowing the audience in sensuality, in movement, and in music, light, and colour.[27]

As Catherine Bell argues, 'The dynamic interaction of texts and rites, reading and chanting, the word fixed and the word preached are practices, not social developments of a fixed nature and significance'.[28] Newson can be configured as a choreographer/theatre maker who 'ritualizes' or 're-vocalizes' psychological and mythic events in a late-twentieth-century mode, capturing these events and reworking them using political and consumerist strategies of the present to reinforce the message by mixing ancient and contemporary voices.

Lloyd Newson is not alone in linking contemporary psychological and Greek material. An honourable history exists in modern dance. As in Martha Graham's work, there is often evidence of the individual making sense of her/his own life and her/his

choreographic work which results in themes of death, eroticism and the maternal body.[29] It might be suggested, rather stereotypically, that for Newson, as an avowedly gay male choreographer, the maternal body is of little *erotic* significance. More to the point, perhaps, is the fear of avenging angels, as in Nigel Charnock's fear of Wendy Houstoun. This draws on an 'almost universal, deeply seated aversion to the female body' which Ramsay Burt attributes to the 'violence and horror of separation' from the mother – a modern psychoanalytic interpretation but one which resonates with Greek obsessions.

An episode embodying this idea appears in the stage version of *Strange Fish*, which is not repeated in the video version, in which Diana Payne-Myers, the older dancer who appears first of all as a frail, nun-like figure, is tossed around by a group of young men, like a doll or a ball. This sadistic entertainment for immature men on a night out suggests the need to establish their difference.

William Beers's demonstration that public rituals of the *current time* continue to be rituals of sacrifice seems useful here.[30] He argues that, since the 'sacred' is socially constructed, the threat of instability is always present.[31] Ritual blood sacrifice is a universal occurrence among patrilineal societies. The intrusion of archaic forms of narcissism, it is believed, is the source of anxiety disorders in the modern world. Rage and aggression are common where the individual perceives the activity of others as 'wounds to the self', not as independent of the self.

It is not unreasonable to suggest that *Strange Fish* can be seen as a ritual of 'blood sacrifice' and, applying Beers's terms, as a *male-identified rite that is gender-specific, and an expression of male narcissistic anxiety*. Sacrifice is understood as an ancient 'male-bonding' ritual, an act of separation from women by means of which men can both bond with each other and appropriate women's power. This seems a more than adequate characterization of Scene 3 in *Strange Fish*.

Strange Fish, however, has relatively little bonding overall. Rather, it exposes trauma and critiques very successfully the uncomfortable nature of society's rituals. Characters are presented as real individuals, not as representations of some named character or as archetypes. This even extends to Wendy Houstoun using Nigel Charnock's real name in moments of *extremis*, just as Nigel addresses individuals by their own names in the party scene. These scenes of social interaction perversely seem to cause distress and discomfort for the performers, and do not 'make safe' dangerous feelings in the way myth is supposed to do.

Occasionally, Wendy and Nigel glimpse the possibility of belonging to a duo or group, but this sense does not last: the fleeting moment of comfort serves only to point up its continuing absence. What it does 'make safe' is another layer which says that it is acceptable at the end of the twentieth century to expose our wildest and most bitter moments, as television chat-shows and confessional and 'reality' series appear to demonstrate. Anything less would be trivial perhaps.

Fin de Siècle: Voices of the Millennium

Strange Fish was extremely popular at the time of its making (1992). It was then televised (1994) and made available on video (BBC/RMArts).[32] It gave rise to extensive comment, although this was largely confined to short articles which neither exhaust the subject nor uncover its multiple layers and complexities. None of the critics made a connection between the subject matter of this piece and the approach of the end of the millennium. In the meantime, however, 'millennium fever' developed commercial symptoms. Religious aspects were considerably lower key, reflecting the diminution of interest in, and of the dominance of, Christianity in the western world, although events based more loosely on religious themes were prominent in certain artistic contexts.

These manifestations lent support to the idea that, while the number of practising churchgoers in the Anglican Church in the UK had sunk to a new low, the story of the life of Jesus Christ and the institution of the Church remained a powerful and enduring part of western mythology. In the 2001 National Census, the results of which have recently been analyzed, 71 per cent of people in this country still describe themselves as Christian.

An American film, *Stigmata* (1999, dir. Rupert Wainwright), tells the story of a girl receiving a rosary from her mother in a remote Brazilian village. The wounds of Christ appear on her body. The legitimacy of the claims made for her, and the involvement of the Vatican, testify to the usefulness of this myth as a set of intertexts. There was an exhibition at the National Gallery in London called *Seeing Salvation: the Image of Christ* (February–May 2000), linked to a BBC TV programme culminating on Easter Sunday. It brought together 79 images of Christ, selected, unlike previous chronological exhibitions, around several themes: 'Sign and Symbol', 'The Dual Nature', 'The True Likeness', 'Passion and Compassion', 'Praying the Passion', 'The Saving Body', and 'The Abiding Presence'.

Harrison Birtwistle's opera was specifically commissioned for 2000. He explored the significance of *The Last Supper* for the third millennium in a series of dramatic tableaux. He recognizes that these are commodified images, already loaded with history, but perhaps no more or less a commodity than they were in the second, fourth, or fifteenth centuries. Recycling myths and adapting them to fit the changing times is a recurrent pastime of ideology-makers, whether they are religious leaders, politicians, composers, choreographers, or art curators.

Dramatic Narrative Tendencies

I turn now to voices from within the text. *Strange Fish* self-consciously asks the reader to address the question of who is telling the story. The narrator is conventionally seen as a reliable, external, prophetic voice. In *Strange Fish*, however, a number of subject positions can be heard in consequence of the actions of the performers.

Scene 1 seems to engage the reader as if from Wendy Houstoun's point of view as she moves around the foot of the cross and behind the penitent figure kneeling in prayer. The singing voice, on the other hand, encourages sympathy with the figure suspended on the cross. In Scene 2, the active subjects are Nigel Charnock and Wendy Houstoun, united in private, inwardly focused social interaction. Despite the increasing number of participants in Scene 3, it is Lauren Potter and Wendy Houstoun who seem to be controlling the viewers' perspective by initiating unpleasant attacks on others. Increasingly, one becomes aware of the camera director, particularly in the rapid movement of Scene 4.

In Scene 5, while sympathy with the lovers is generated, the fact that Wendy is watching, cynically, from the foreground cannot be ignored, since she usurps the viewer's position. From the start of Scene 6, there is an atmosphere of waiting for something to happen as at a party. Nigel enters babbling into this sociable but rather unfocused gathering. From then on, his level of anxiety puts one directly in his position. This is intensified in Scene 7, in close-focused events where Nigel attempts to force his way between other couples. Wendy's slap on his face, when she forces him away, feels like a slap in our own.

In Scene 9, where Wendy and Melanie are present (the latter in the role of the Angel), the narrator's role seems to reside more with Melanie as observer of the futility of human intercourse. Melanie's position also seems to focus Scene 11 as she supports the sick figure, here again in the role of the Angel.

Narrative voices can be perceived not only in the position of narrator but also in the location of scenes. The church scenes are two in number in *Strange Fish*, strategically placed to set the mood and to create a sense of opening up the work and then closing it. The very framework of a church calls up notions of dignity and humility, reverence and recognition of one's insignificance, belief and prayer (rather than agnosticism and atheism), and judgement.

The most obvious and immediate contrast between the first and last scenes is in the atmosphere and mood. The bar scenes (Scenes 3 and 4, and then the party scene, Scene 6), emphasize sociability, desirability, mixing with others, meeting and parting, competitiveness, personal success and distress. The original bar scene becomes a party scene illu-minated by coloured lights, and the emphasis shifts from small groups to the larger group. The corridor scenes (Scenes 2, 5, 8, and 10) draw on a different set of texts. Corridors are places for casual meetings, for passing others with barely a glance, or for furtive, secretive, and intimate moments. There is an element of danger in the narrowness of corridors, the possibility of confrontation, and the threat of not being able to escape easily.

Each scene carries different significance within this agenda, as the title and subsequent action reveal. The idea of corridors, perceived as places of potential threat, binds Scenes 8 to 10, whereas Scenes 2 and 5 emphasize more positive and enjoyable aspects of relationships in corridors. While a *bar* is an open environment from which escape is possible, and a corridor explicitly raises the question of escape, some other smaller rooms carry a more intense message. Scenes 7, 9 and 11 take place in intimate settings, the first in a social space, but one confined by the use of lighting, the second in a 'bedroom', and the third around the sides of a water tank in an enclosed space. There is greater possibility in these environments for deep and genuine communication, whether agonized or joyful.

Individual Voices

The spaces which the video creates set the scene for individual action. Wendy Houstoun takes the role of the quintessential observer and malicious influence. She is often alone and alienated, but makes constant efforts to disrupt the relationships of others and to manipulate outcomes, as in the bar scenes. Her own attempts at intimacy always seem to be doomed. First conniving with Lauren Potter and then attempting to destroy her is one of Wendy's specialities.

In Scene 4, Molina's self-absorbed sensuality is shattered by Wendy's and Lauren's predatory, circling, teasing game. It is Lauren who succumbs to the male in this disturbing piece, not Wendy, here or ever. Group relationships reveal the underlying individual voices of desperation. Their interactions range in tone from the compulsive emotional dependency of Lauren and Jordi getting together in

Scene 4 to the compulsive, mindless sex of Wendy and Dale in Scene 9, and the utterly terrifying demonstration of emotional need between Wendy and Nigel, which ends in violence (Scene 10).

Even loving consolation is marred by the bittersweet sadness in Scene 11 of baptism and absolution between Melanie as 'Angel' and Dale, the dying sufferer. Intimidation and competition (Scene 3), with the group lending approval, is compounded by the party (Scene 6), where deeply unkind acts continue. Neither is there mercy or sympathy or pity, as Scene 9's aftermath of sex is judged by the group. The ultimate betrayal is the Judas kiss that Wendy forces on Christ – Melanie – since it leads to death.

Conclusion

It is often argued that the Christian message is described as universal not because everyone believes it but *because* of its successful assimilation of the pre-Christian religious heritage – the Cross as the tree of life, the ritual use of wine – as well as its continuous use over two thousand years. Ancient stories about fish are also inherited. Tales of Hindu and Chinese goddesses, known as fish goddesses, were the precursors of the penis-swallowing Kali, also known as Minaksi (the fish-eyed). Swallowing genitals and giving birth to rivers – and gods – is a significant way not only of expressing the fears of the male (as Freudian commentators suggest), but also of conferring greater power and dignity on the male, mainly by appropriating features particular to women.[33]

Less violent, but still common in many western cultures, is the practice of eating fish on Fridays, recalling the orgiastic fish-eating goddess Salacia. James Davidson argues that the Greeks were passionately fond of fish, which amounted to a dominant obsession in fourth-century discourses.[34] A twist to this story is that the fish involved in this literal or metaphorical seduction may have been a source of occult power, as well as being as 'mouth-watering' as women. Nothing is so simple, however. Interpretations of fish madness may have been ironic, since the appre-

ciation of fish – in contrast to the public, sacrificial position of animals – was part of a private and modern discourse of connoisseurship. Comedy at that time included shopping lists, fish menus, and recipes.

The intertextual point is that the texts relevant to *Strange Fish* have traces of the immediate present, as well as of the supposedly dead past. If it is obvious that 'all texts contain traces of other texts', then a more sophisticated version of this idea draws attention to 'the interactions between texts, producers of texts and their readers' lifeworlds'.[35]

There are several threads of intertextuality and of gender politics operating within the work. Each of these referential strands, and their interactions, are compounded by my own response to the 'texts' that are *Strange Fish*. They illustrate both the constraints on interpretation and the potential for endless reinterpretation. Paradoxically, intertextuality allows the reader to 'create the text' and, simultaneously, to 'read the text as it wishes to be read'.[36] Or, expressed in another way, it is 'a tool which cannot be employed by readers wishing to produce stability and order, or wishing to claim authority over the text or other critics', but one which continuously opens up possibilities of reading.[37]

Notes and References

1. I have published a chapter specifically on the musical landscape as 'Siren Sensualities in Physical Theatre: Lloyd Newson's *Strange Fish* (1992)', in Linda Austern, ed., *Music, Sensation, and Sensuality*, Critical and Cultural Musicology, Vol 5 (New York; London: Routledge, 2002), p. 121–36.

2. The use of the term 'ancestral' does not imply here that the relevant texts are necessarily old, although some are.

3. Theoretical underpinnings can be found in the following: Janet Adshead-Lansdale, ed., *Dancing Texts: Intertextuality in Interpretation* (London: Dance Books, 1999); Graham Allen, *Intertextuality* (London; New York: Routledge, 2000); Umberto Eco, The *Role of the Reader: Explorations in the Semiotics of Texts* (Bloomington: Indiana, 1979, 1984); Marco De Marinis, *The Semiotics of Performance* (Bloomington: Indiana, 1993); and Michael Worton and Judith Still, ed., *Intertextuality: Theories and Practices* (Manchester: Manchester University Press, 1990).

4. EDT was one of the small companies to emerge, at the Edinburgh Festival in 1975 from the burst of activity at The Place which followed the first performances of London Contemporary Dance Theatre in 1967. EDT became a well-respected middle-scale

company. Emilyn Claid's appointment as Artistic Director in 1981 heralded a change of direction towards experimental dance and to politically charged work. Newson produced *Breaking Images* in 1982, *Beauty, Art, and the Kitchen Sink* in 1984, and three workshop pieces in 1983 and 1984 for EDT.

5. Andy Solway, 'Lloyd Newson interview' *New Dance*, No. 34 (Autumn 1985), p. 10–11. A more extended account of the works produced by the company, their subject matter, and treatment, can be found on the company website www.dv8.co.uk.

6. As in the work of de Valois for the Royal Ballet and Cohan for London Contemporary Dance Theatre.

7. Fiona Burnside, 'Home Thoughts from Abroad', *Dance Theatre Journal*, IX, No. 3 (Spring 1992), p. 30–3, 42.

8. More recent analyses of Butcher's and Davies's work can be found in Libby Worth and Sophia Preston's articles respectively, both in Janet Adshead-Lansdale, ed., *Dancing Texts: Intertextuality in Interpretation* (London: Dance Books, 1999).

9. The criteria on which Burnside bases her stylistic judgements emerge and, of course, the weakness of attempting generalizations in a modernist, individualistic dance form become clear. However, it is a worthwhile exercise in that similarities and differences do emerge, while even the most individualistic dance-makers can be seen to emerge from specific local and cultural contexts.

10. Sophie Constanti, 'Easing the Load', *Dance Theatre Journal*, V, No. 2 (Summer 1998), p. 26–9.

11. More recent analyses of Anderson's work can be found in Dodds, in Adshead-Lansdale., ed., 1999.

12. 'Dance on the Edge', *Dance Now*, V. No. 4 (Winter 1996–7), p. 67–75.

13. It is easy to criticize this attempt to classify work, and these categories would not stand up to detailed analytic scrutiny; but Parry's reflections embody the view of the time as well as a critical attempt to sort out the many emerging trends.

14. Lloyd Newson, 'Lloyd Newson about *Strange Fish*', *Dance and Dancers* , July 1992, p. 10–13.

15. In this he has been likened to Pina Bausch, Jan Fabre, and other European choreographers of recent years.

16. Patricia Grayburn, ed., *Gertrud Bodenwieser 1890–1959* (Guildford: University of Surrey, 1990).

17. Jann Parry, 'Outside Dance', *Dance Theatre Journal*, VIII, No. 3 (Autumn 1990), p. 43.

18. On inspection, references to him starting with a scenario or score or narrative in *Strange Fish* reveal a very cursory document with no more than brief outlines of scenes.

19. See, for example, Nadine Meisner, 'Strange Fish', *Dance and Dancers*, July 1992, p. 10–13; 'Lloyd Newson on . . . Dance', *Dance Now*, II, No. 2 (Summer 1993), p. 11–13; Jann Parry, 'Strange Fish', *Dance Now*, I, No. 3 (Autumn 1992), p. 22–7; Andy Solway, 'Lloyd Newson Interview' *New Dance*, No. 34 (Autumn 1985), p. 10–11.

20. Dennis O'Toole, 'Raw Fish', *The List*, Glasgow, 5–18 June 1992.

21. Nadine Meisner, 'Strange Fish', *Dance and Dancers*, July 1992, p. 10–13.

22. Jann Parry, 'Strange Fish', *Dance Now*, I, No. 3 (Autumn 1992), p. 22–7.

23. Nadine Meisner, 'Strange Fish', *Dance and Dancers*, July 1992, p. 10–13.

24. 'Lloyd Newson on . . . Dance', *Dance Now,* II, No. 2 (Summer 1993), p. 11–13.

25. Pook is a member of '3 or 4 Composers' and 'Elektra Strings'. This latter group of six women work on music performance/theatre projects as well as pop bands. She has worked with Eurythmics, the Communards, the Manic Street Preachers, Meat Loaf, the Stranglers, and Style Council. Her commissions for DV8 include *My Body, Your Body* (1988); *MSM* (1994); and for 'O Vertigo Dance Company', *Deluge* (1994). Pappenheim's musical experiences, first as a choral scholar at King's, London, have taken her across Europe and have covered Lieder, early music, and Kurt Weill.

26. The lament still flourishes in folk forms in Mediterranean areas in Europe, e.g., in Hungary.

27. Rather than affirming 'clear and dogmatic values . . . ritual actually constructs an argument, a set of tensions' (Catherine Bell, *Ritual Theory, Ritual Practice* Oxford: Oxford University Press, 1992, p. 145); and it does this on its own terms, in its own language, not pretending to be something else. It is this perspective that resonates with *Strange Fish.*

28. Catherine Bell, *Ritual Theory, Ritual Practice* (Oxford: Oxford University Press, 1992).

29. Ramsay Burt, 'Dance, Gender, and Psychoanalysis', *Dance Research Journal*, XXX, No. 21 (Spring 1998), p. 30–3, 42.

30. On the symbolic in culture, William Beers uses the work of Mary Douglas and Victor Turner, and in particular the articulation of 'structural conflicts and contradictions, which symbols initiate, conceal, and transform', while criticizing the absence of a psychodynamic position in work of this kind. William Beers, *Women and Sacrifice: Male Narcissism and the Psychology of Religion* (Detroit: Wayne State University Press, 1992), p. 40.

31. As Mary Douglas argues, in *Purity and Danger* (London: Routledge, 1966), all social systems can be seen to be 'at war with themselves'.

32. Lloyd Newson and David Hinton, *Strange Fish* (BBC/RMArts video, 1994).

33. Jan Bremmer, *Interpretation of Greek Mythology* (Australia: Croom Helm, 1987).

34. James Davidson, *Courtesans and Fishcakes: the Consuming Passions of Classical Athens* (London: Fontana, 1998).

35. Ulrike Meinhof and Jonathan Smith, ed., *Intertextuality and the Media* (Manchester: Manchester University Press, 2000).

36. Umberto Eco, *The Role of the Reader: Explorations in the Semiotics of Texts* (Bloomington: Indiana University Press, 1979, 1984).

37. Graham Allen, *Intertextuality* (London; New York: Routledge, 2000).

Laurence Senelick

Stanislavsky's Second Thoughts on 'The Seagull'

Stanislavsky's first production of *The Seagull* is well documented in English, in *The Seagull Produced by Stanislavsky*, edited by S. D. Balukhaty in 1952. But little is known of his exploratory work on an intended second production almost two decades later amidst the turmoil of the revolutionary period, and the rehearsal notes made by Stanislavsky's assistant Pyotr Sharov remained unpublished even in Russian until 1987. Here, Laurence Senelick provides the first English translation of these notes, contextualizing them with an account of the difficulties under which Stanislavsky and the Art Theatre were working at the time. Laurence Senelick is Fletcher Professor of Drama and Oratory at Tufts University, and a long-time contributor to TQ and NTQ, which published his articles on the Craig–Stanislavsky *Hamlet*, serf theatre in Russia, and Wedekind and Lenin at the music hall. His last book, *The Changing Room: Sex, Drag, and Theatre*, won the George Jean Nathan award as the best work of dramatic criticism of 2000–01, and his previous book, *The Chekhov Theatre: a Century of Plays in Production*, won the Barnard Hewitt award of the American Society of Theatre Research. He is currently translating and editing the complete plays and dramatic fragments of Anton Chekhov for Norton Publishers.

FOR THE RUSSIAN EMPIRE 1916 was a disastrous year. Its participation in the First World War had been calamitous, with four million men killed over the twelve-month period. Ill-equipped and incompetently commanded, the regular army evaporated, and the Germans overran Russian Poland. The government was in disarray: Rasputin, whose interference had exacerbated the tensions between the Imperial family and the administration, was finally assassinated in December. Refugees were streaming into Moscow and St Petersburg; food queues lengthened, leading to bread riots; the suicide rate tripled.

Much as it tried to keep itself above the fray, the Moscow Art Theatre vibrated to the uncertainty and anxiety of the times. The usually strained relations between Stanislavsky and his partner Nemirovich-Danchenko came near to breaking point, and new productions were few. In 1915, an evening of Pushkin one-acts had been poorly received by the critics, and over the next season two plays of contemporary life, Surguchev's *Autumn Violins* and Merezhkovsky's *Let There Be Joy*, failed to engage theatregoers. For the first time in twelve years, the theatre did not tour to St Petersburg. In the 1916–17 season, the First Studio, where young actors were experimenting with Stanislavsky's system of acting, confined its public presentation to an evening of Chekhov sketches.

In January 1916 Stanislavsky had proposed that *The Seagull* – which had received only sixty-three performances between its opening in 1898 and its excision from the repertory in 1905 – be revived, employing many members of the original cast. The idea had to be postponed when, that same month, he began directing Nemirovich's adaptation of Dostoevsky's novella *The Village of Stepanchikovo*. Stanislavsky was also to play the leading role of Rostanev, the landowner victimized by a hypocritical hanger-on.

At this stage in his thinking, he was beginning to emphasize action over emotion as the driving force in an actor's creativity. He regarded the rehearsals for *Stepanchikovo* as an opportunity to explore these new ideas about creative technique, an approach which would enable the actor to interpret a character more fully and to penetrate the 'artist's paradise' of living-through a part. In addition to these duties, however, he was also playing such leading roles as Vershinin, Gaev, and Satin in the regular repertory, doing sporadic work on Aleksandr Blok's verse drama *The Rose and the Cross*, and occasionally visiting rehearsals of the Second Studio's opening production, Zinaida Gippius's play of modern youth, *The Green Ring*.

Meanwhile, political events had caused an industrial dispute at his factory and a walk-out of stagehands at the theatre. And in December Stanislavsky's close associate and disciple, Leopold Sulerzhitsky, who was chiefly responsible for the work of the First Studio, died of tuberculosis.

Amidst this turmoil – political, professional, emotional – work on *Stepanchikovo* dragged on through 150 rehearsals, and while those who saw Stanislavsky's passive, even Christ-like Rostanev, were impressed, he could not come to closure. February 1917 saw two revolutions: one took place in the streets and overturned the monarchy; the other occurred when Nemirovich-Danchenko took over as director of the Dostoevsky play. The two partners immediately locked horns over the interpretation of the leading role. On 28 March 1917, after the dress rehearsal, Stanislavsky gave up the part.

What he had experienced with Rostanev he would later call his 'tragedy'. It deeply shook his self-confidence as an actor, and from that time on he refrained from taking on new roles (except to play the secondary part of Prince Shuisky in *Tsar Fyodor* on tour). When *The Village of Stepanchikovo* opened the theatre's twentieth season on 26 September 1917, the directors' names were not on the programme.

The Cast of the Production

Such were the circumstances under which Stanislavsky set out to re-direct *The Seagull*. By the late August of 1917, when he began to schedule work on the play, he was still reeling not only from the *Stepanchikovo* trauma but from political events – Kerensky's Provisional Government was now shakily installed. With his factories and even his house taken over by the state, Stanislavsky was dependent on his private resources. He determined

to concentrate on the 'aesthetic realm', and to use art to educate 'the people's sensibility, their souls'. *The Seagull*, he now believed, was about devotion to art. Submersion in Chekhov's play seems to have been a kind of refuge, in which nostalgia for one of the Art Theatre's great successes was overshadowed by his desire to create something fresh, youthful, and vigorous.

Of the original cast, only Olga Knipper was enlisted into the new production. When she had first played Arkadina in 1898, she had been only thirty, a recent graduate of the Moscow Philharmonic, too young and inexperienced for the part. Now forty-nine, the widow of Anton Chekhov, and an established 'star' of the Art Theatre, she could serve as an anchor for the company.

The rest of the new cast was deliberately made up either of very young actors, seasoned only by work in the studios, or relatively minor players, who had yet to be entrusted with major assignments in the parent company. Nina, considered by Stanislavsky to be the central role, was to be doubled by Alla Tarasova and Olga Baklanova. Tarasova, a plump, dark-eyed brunette, had caught Stanislavsky's eye in the Second Studio's *Green Ring*. In the Soviet period, she would become a leading actress of the MAT and a favourite of Stalin's; but at this point she was still a raw tyro.

Baklanova, a svelte blonde, had played nothing but servant-girls on the main stage, until entrusted with Luisa in *The Feast in Plaguetime* and Laura in *The Stone Guest* in the Pushkin evening. Her best performance, however, had been in the First Studio, as the streetwalker Lizzie in Berger's *The Flood*. She too would come into her own after the Revolution, as the leading actress in Nemirovich's Musical Studio; she would remain in the US after a tour, gravitate to Hollywood, and win enduring notoriety as the venal acrobat in Todd Browning's *Freaks*.

Responsibility for Treplyov was invested in Mikhail (Michael) Chekhov, partnered by the newcomer Grigory Yudin. Chekhov, a nephew of the writer, had entered the Art Theatre in 1912, and from the start Stanislavsky had tried to instil in him the principles of his system. In the intimate surroundings of the First Studio, Chekhov's performances as Caleb Plummer in *Cricket on the Hearth* and Frazer in *The Flood* had been outstanding. Stanislavsky entrusted him with playing Epikhodov in *The Cherry Orchard*, encouraging him to make the character idiosyncratic to himself. He regarded Chekhov primarily as a comic talent, and doubted his abilities in tragedy, a doubt which was confirmed in the 1920s, when Chekhov played Hamlet. In rehearsing the young actor as Treplyov, Stanislavsky tried to encourage him, through the character, to believe in himself.

Of the other characters, Masha was assigned to Mariya Kryzhanovskaya, a recent arrival in the Art Theatre, whose main responsibility so far had been as Rostanev's daughter Nastenka in *The Village of Stepanchikovo*. Trigorin, which had been Stanislavsky's part, was to be played by Konstantin Khokhlov, a character actor of some range, who had been seen as the moronic Greek Purikes in *Anathema*, the district prosecutor in *The Brothers Karamazov*, and Horatio in the Gordon Craig *Hamlet*. Pyotr Baksheev, the new Shamraev, had been a useful character man since 1911, but was rarely entrusted with substantial roles.

Dr Dorn was to be Aleksey Stakhovich, a former major-general and adjutant to the Governor General of Moscow, who had, after his retirement, become a stockholder and a patron of the Art Theatre. The starchy, bemonocled officer began as a standby for Stanislavsky and worked in the Second Studio. Vladimir Neronov, the new Sorin, had joined the Art Theatre only in 1916, and was untested. Vera Pavlova, the new Polina Andreevna, though she had been a charter member of the Art Theatre since 1898, rarely played anything but small, nameless roles.

Hatching a New Gull

In other words, the cast, for the most part, was inexperienced or, as Stanislavsky saw it, unspoiled either by routine or by exposure to conventional methods of acting. All of them had received their training or their stage skills within the Art Theatre. The vitality and vigour of such promising talents as Tarasova and Mikhail Chekhov would aid Stanislavsky in bringing out the theme of devotion to art.

Work on *The Seagull* proceeded over the course of five months, from September of that year to June 1918, the very period when the October Revolution put the Bolsheviks in power, the seeds of Civil War were sown, and famine began to be felt in the cities.[1] None of these outside events finds a place in Stanislavsky's comments, for, typically, he used his absorption in rehearsals to block out the unpleasant realities of everyday life. His new vision of Chekhov and the play emphasized high spirits, activity, and courage. It was to serve as a therapeutic remedy for the woes he and his society were suffering. Hence the stress on youth and youthful feelings and the repeated emphasis on moments of joy, humour, and faith.

There is a world of difference between Stanislavsky's work on *The Seagull* in 1898 and that of 1917. In 1898, faced with a troupe of novices and amateurs, he left nothing to the actor's imagination, but laid down everything in his marginal glosses. As I have written elsewhere, 'Stanislavsky "through-composed" the text, setting it to details of mood.' The 'score' for the first Art Theatre production (which is available in an English translation of Sergey Balukhaty's edition published in 1952) is compendious: every gesture, from lighting a cigarette to moving a lamp, is prescribed, atmospheric effects are heavily laid on, pauses are inlaid, and intonations are described. As is well known, Stanislavsky confessed that he did not understand the play, and so, to make it a success in a failing season, he used it as a pretext for directorial invention.

In 1917, it was another story. *The Seagull* was now part of the Art Theatre legend and served as its emblem and mascot. A 'Chekhovian' style of acting had accreted, and a lamentable tendency to indulge in 'moaning and groaning' (*nytyo*) had set in. Stanislavsky was eager to clear away all the preconceptions about how to play Chekhov. To this end, he insisted on highly energized, buoyant acting, and, most important, on the actors' discovering for themselves their characters' states of mind. The behavioural details that dominated in the earlier production are now abandoned in favour of psychological states and their nuances. He even urges Neronov to ignore Sorin's illness, lest details of physical degeneration vitiate the main traits of the character.

Similarly, he downplays the romantic aspect of the play. Nina, he tells Tarasova, is not in love with Kostya but with the stage. Their love scene in the first act is the result of circumstance and awkwardness. Five years later, in his memoir *My Life in Art*, written for an American audience he considered naive, Stanislavsky would describe *The Seagull* in terms of a love story. Within the Russian context, however, he insisted that love for art trumps personal relations.

Even as he insists that the actors must identify and 'treasure' the 'salient word' at every moment, Stanislavsky points out that Chekhov is not Ostrovsky, and the lines alone cannot convey the meaning of what is going on. The words designate underlying meanings, and it is these inner meanings – the characters' mental states – which have to be ascertained and conveyed to the spectator. Each scene, episode, or line has to be examined to decipher the concealed *leitmotivs* of each role and the play in general.

In applying his system in rehearsals, Stanislavsky used a vocabulary which is familiar to us now, but at the time was newly minted. He has the actors break the play down into *kuski* (literally, pieces). Elizabeth Reynolds Hapgood's widely disseminated version of his writings renders this as 'units', but I have chosen to translate it as *segments*. At times he metaphorized small segments as *beads* (*busy*), which have to be strung together.[2] He regularly refers to the *zadacha*, which I translate as *problem* (like a sum in

---

The Rehearsal Notes[3]
10 September 1917

Analysis of Act Three

Analyzes Nina's attitude to Treplyov's recent suicide attempt.

Then K. S. in passing addresses all the performers: that after the last rehearsal they were '*warming up*' to their roles.

Popov as Medvedenko has a somewhat pessimistic mood.

Tarasova is getting stronger in the role and is eager to rehearse.

[Mikhail] Chekhov does not want to get bogged down in a detailed breakdown of the role, because he has not yet had time to grasp the role as a whole.

Neronov is still unclear about Sorin's attitude to his sister.

K. S. advises [Neronov] to forget about [Sorin's] illness. All this has to be pushed into the background. It interferes with the major, basic lines of the role. It's very detrimental to steer a characterization in the direction of infirmity.

K. S. talks about how Treplyov, though nervous, is not a neurotic. We have to show his courage, the strength of his convictions about his ideas. He is a fighter. His characterization is to be a man firm in his convictions.

The previous rehearsal achieved a great deal for Baksheev. His role came closer.

K. S. asks them not to forget, to analyze the nature of their feelings. They must not forget the silent moments, when others are speaking, and they only listen.

Stakhovich is somewhat embarrassed by his personal tendency to speak with a kind of sneer. Private rehearsals with V. L. Mchedelov[4] have been a great help in this regard.

Pavlova continues to be perplexed and cannot find the essence of 'sloppy sentimentality'.

O. L. Knipper is trying for a frivolous 'actor's tone'.

K. S. advises her [to base herself] on real-life observations of old performers, their way of speaking.

They have begun to read the first act from the entrance of Treplyov and Sorin.

Sorin's first line is not right. He has to speak it as *usual*, and not as if for the first time. It follows that even Kostya must restrain [his uncle's] usual 'maundering'. Otherwise it will come across as the beginning of a scene. It has to be the continuation of a scene, and not the beginning. Even here one has to pick the salient word to be

mathematics), to be solved in each phase of the action. (Hapgood popularized the term *objective* in this regard; Jean Benedetti translates it more literally as *task*.)

Given circumstances (*predlagaemye obstoyatelsta*) represent the situation in which the characters find themselves. *Through-action* (*skvoznoe deystvie*, or what Hapgood calls the 'through line of action') connects all the actions of a character and progresses towards the character's ultimate goal. He also makes a distinction between 'activity' (*aktivnost*) and 'action' (*deystvie*). At this point he is asking the actors to try to find the *key* (*klyuch*) to a segment, but later abandoned that term.

Unfortunately, the 'given circumstances' surrounding the rehearsals were not propitious. Material living conditions in Moscow grew worse. Mikhail Chekhov fell ill, as did Tarasova. In May 1918 she took a leave of absence and left famine-ridden Moscow to recover in the well-provisioned Ukraine; in August she informed the administration that she would not be back in time for the beginning of the fall season. Rehearsals of *The Seagull* were discontinued. In January 1919, Tarasova wrote to Stanislavsky that it was 'the dream of my life' to play Nina, and that she had every intention of doing so 'without fail, at any cost'. It was not to be. In the event, the Art Theatre was not to restage *The Seagull* until Oleg Efremov completely rethought the play in 1980.

Of the rehearsals Stanislavsky held for the *Seagull* revival, only four sets of notes have survived. They were made by the assistant director Pyotr Sharov, who, later, as Peter Sharoff, became a prominent Chekhov director in Italy and the Netherlands. They were first published by the chronicler of Stanislavsky's life I. N. Vinogradskaya in 1987, and appear here in English for the first time.

---

stressed. 'Somehow's *not the thing*?' You mustn't make automatic emphases.

With time you have to attain a high level of temperament in this role [Treplyov]. You must restrain your gestures. Especially [Mikhail] Chekhov's tiny gestures, which appear to be his sole inadequacy for this role.

The more restrained the gestures, the more powerful the temperament.

'Underacting' simplicity always comes about when people don't appreciate the precious, salient words. That is the old Art Theatre – to act simplicity is the worst, most appalling cliché.

Without kindliness there is no Sorin. He is not *calm*, but kindly, lively, interested in everything.

K. S. Stanislavsky's remarks.

[Mikhail] Chekhov's seriousness was evident, but his high spirits disappeared. There was no joy, no faith. They have begun to 'act' [Anton] Chekhov. That's awful. They turned a performance into a funeral.

Shamraev has to be even more serious, authoritative. The stage of the old theatre is his 'holy of holies'. He has to talk with the 'feelings' of a theatre buff, and not illustrate the words.

Neronov still doesn't have enough merriment and kindliness.

Pavlova has nothing but sloppy sentimentality. In her joys, her jealousies, everything – sloppy sentimentality.

Dorn is always inwardly cheerful, wise. His eyes are joyful. Without any strain. He even regards her affectionately, cheerfully.

Tarasova has forgotten about [Treplyov's] play, the house has very much polluted her. Today this is a plus.

The first act went up to [the beginning of Treplyov's] play. Everyone is looking for the right direction, many new things happened and earlier discoveries have been set aside; and this is very good. In the end everything will coalesce: all the 'beads' will be strung.

They went on to the second act. They read as far as Nina's soliloquy. Then they begin to analyze what's been read.

Arkadina is the only one who isn't depressed. She's all energy. Taken up with herself. Other people's attention still gets her worked up. Masha is struggling with what is dragging her down; she is suffering, but takes herself in hand. Dorn is living his own life. He hums – that's the nicest thing about the role.

Arkadina's energy is analogous to Savina's energy and liveliness. K. S. tells a story about a performance at his home at Red Gates. How everyone left [worn out and how Fedotova] was high-spirited and merry.[5] She's a firecracker.

Sorin has a joyful smile, and not the 'routine' actor's smile, which does not admit seriousness. Sorin is very fond of Nina. He is happy when she's happy. Is he attracted to Nina? More accurately, it's a fondness for youth.

'I'm happy' – this line [of Nina's] contains both sadness and happiness. How quickly it has come, how soon it will pass. Youth is dust.

Is Arkadina jealous of Nina on account of Trigorin? Arkadina notices her outburst. She is jealous. Nina's arrival upsets her.

Her son interested her. [Arkadina] thinks about him seriously.

Masha warns Arkadina about Kostya: 'He's very downhearted.'

'Recite his poetry or something from his play' – this is connected with her torment over the last few days. She's all about Kostya, and all her lines connect to her love for Kostya. And then once more she 'dons her toga'.

'All that is so uninteresting' – it's a betrayal of Kostya. How can she do it? She, so young, so noble? She does it very delicately, gently: 'Do I have to recite?' can be heard in [Nina's] refusal.

Here Masha is full of bravado. She wants to show that he [Treplyov] is a genius, a poet.

Why does she ask 'timidly'? K. S. thinks that it is, rather, thoughtfulness, and, perhaps, the result of their strained relations. A bit of jealousy.

Shamraev arrives 'to relax' among actors, at whom he immediately starts to yell. A kind of emotional outburst that can take place only in a heat wave.

Arkadina here reveals all that's worst in her actress's nature. Nina, affected by the scandal, the general agitation – gets excited herself and is genuinely outraged by Shamraev. Sorin starts to shout at the end of the scene because he's been frightened, like an 'old biddy'.

Nina goes into utter despair over what's happening in the house.

Polina's jealousy.

Nina alone. She is completely defeated. Her great naivety. You have to reveal her assumptions about life. Treplyov enters [with the killed seagull].

They read the third act.

Remarks.

Chekhovian moaning and groaning.

Arkadina's stinginess. She clutches at whatever's cheapest and gradually refuses everything. The psychology of stinginess in Arkadina. One rouble for three servants. Sorin [talking to her about money] is very candid, not chiding Arkadina. She joyously launches into memories of her youth. In the quarrel with her son she hams it up, and then immediately turns into a cook. An instant more – and she is transformed into the kindest of women. It's all very sincere, with an actor's temperament, it's all overblown, and therefore all the feelings are exaggerated.

Trigorin? A bit of a coward. In Nina and Trigorin there's a reticence and a hope that something will delay the departure. In the whole scene there's great activity.

In the scene of Arkadina and Trigorin some scene from a tragedy is being played out, and with such effrontery, flattery, that it goes right to Trigorin's head and he cannot struggle.

12 September 1917

V. L. Mchedelov reports on the last rehearsal, specific concerns.

K. S. analyzes the third act, the scene between Treplyov and his mother, makes an analogy between Hamlet and Treplyov. Both are at a time of life when they have nothing in their life except their mother. The dearer she is to them at this moment, the more they want to reform her. The more they will restrain themselves. He decided to commit suicide not because he didn't want to live, but because he passionately wants to live, he grasps at everything that offers a foothold in life, but everything collapses. For him, an aesthete, there is nothing in life that could hold him. His through-action is *to live*, to live beautifully – to aspire to Moscow, to Moscow.[6]

Chekhov is always active. He is not a pessimist – life in the 'eighties was the way that Chekhov's characters created it. He himself loves life, strives for a better life, as do all his characters.

A question for Trigorin/Khokhlov. In order to ascertain the correct problem, one must recall the correct state of mind. The better, the more smoothly the rehearsals proceed, the more profoundly one must consider and ascertain the problem 'by means of the salient word'.

A question for Arkadina/Knipper. The scene with Treplyov and Trigorin. All her psychology is very complicated.

About Tarasova

Is there something getting in the way of the role?

Do you want to rehearse the first act?

What is there about it that frightens the actors?

This is a terrible thing to work with. One must come up with a serious attitude to circumstances, to a mother, to art.

You mustn't reinforce the role with 'gimmicks'. It's a natural habit for performers, which they have to break themselves of.

You have to get excited by the clash of passions. Forget about the external form, if you need something to hold on to, then for the time being you have to say that he is courageous, and how does this show itself now?

The main problem for the performer (Mikhail Chekhov) of the role has to be self-confidence.

With Sorin (Neronov) for some reason nothing new is developing.

With Shamraev (Baksheev) things are doubtful. An agonizing period for Baksheev's talent – it's getting swallowed up by clichés. You have to go back to your original condition (before *Wandering Minstrels*),[7] when there were no clichés.

With Dorn the work is going in an interesting way in the sense of finding the inner essence of the role. A. A. Stakhovich is gradually pulling away from his own personal characteristics, which interfere with the work.

Of Krizhanovskaya

You have to find a 'pose', but not literally. Krizhanovskaya objects, stating that [Masha] is always sincere, really likes taking snuff.

After short discussions we moved from the third act to the second act.

Act II

There's something of Astrov in Dorn. He somehow lives wholly within himself. Sees everything, understands everything. What is Dorn living off of in the second act? To create stage action, we have to find an activity. There's no way to live the 'heat' of the second act. That's not an activity, only a mood.

Sorin has an activity in Act II, 'thirsting for life', which is why he's so happy around Nina.

For Baksheev: he [Shamraev] has come to make trouble either because he's cross, or an oppressive 'life' is eating away at him, and he comes to talk about 'art'. . . .

They begin to read the second act.

After reading the act K. S. poses them all a question: 'Where who how did you feel?'

Baksheev could not control himself and got excited.

[Mikhail] Chekhov did not feel the truth.

Tarasova at the start of the act felt bad, but then it became easy and by the end she was quite in control of herself.

Khokhlov felt comfortable.

K.S. The basic problem of the act?

KHOKHLOV. To please Nina.

K.S. Did you succeed?

[KHOKHLOV]. At moments. The joke, the talk about youth.

KRIZHANOVSKAYA – doesn't feel the role. She was reading lines.

K. S. Aren't [we winding up with] two Ninas?

Masha [in contradistinction to Nina] doesn't reveal her feelings, her lyricism. Maybe, somewhere alone in the moonlight she will open her heart to herself, but immediately gets embarrassed. She is very homely, with a vast fund of feminine lyricism.

A hot summer's day. The residents sit around in a sour mood. In this stagnant society [unexpectedly there appears] a sophisticated actress, 'M. G. Savina'.[8] She makes merry, which is easy for her.

This is the picture you have to come to love, to delineate. No feminine image, the subtlety of competing with young people.

K. S. suggests they 'shape' this scene.

Are they bored or not? They're bored. The eternal Chekhovian theme. People want to leave this boredom of life. In order to strive towards life, there has to be 'boredom', which should make one pull away from this tedious, uninteresting life.

To express lyricism one must give [?] and use the whole range of the voice. A general fault of the theatre is to express lyricism only by a certain lowering and raising of the voice. That's boring.

K.S. suggests they simply do an exercise, he wants to get them on stage. We have lost life. We all need to find it. Meanwhile this pressure, actor's temperament, but no artistic depiction.

Nina is a young girl, whose excitement at meeting Trigorin is almost comic.

To create naivety, one needs a naive frame of mind. For her Trigorin is Shakespeare. Nina respects Trigorin the way A. K. Tarasova respects Shakespeare.

We should [along with Nina] smile at meeting Trigorin. It's all so naive, so overwrought.

It has to be clear to us that she is taking what glitters to be gold, and we should want to shout at her: 'You're making a mistake. You are worth more than any of these celebrities!'

Her coming to this house of celebrities – it's Tyltyl and Mylyll coming to the 'kingdom of unborn souls'.[9]

Treplyov: does he have to go right out and shoot himself or not?

We have to create the picture: a happy young girl, and enter a suicide. Why did he come here, why did he kill the seagull? A man without any reins to steer by. His soul has been emptied out. Nina instinctively feels something tragic in this dramatic figure, and when such individual artistic segments are created along the line of life, the result is tragedy.

We don't have to come up with the result of the whole scene.

We have to come up with a series of life-like phases, otherwise there will [only] be the result, it won't be interesting. In Chekhov the words are the last thing – he's not Ostrovsky. We have to look for original feelings.

Heat. In exercises we might find the true nature of feelings in a heat wave. At first find what external adjustments there are.

K.S. himself plays an exercise without words: 'Heat.' We immediately know the results only too well.

Everyone comes on stage and plays the exercise, improvisations on 'heat'.

K.S. advises they seek the truth not with actors' devices: if you have to portray boredom, then the actor spends the whole scene 'down in the mouth'; if the scene is high-spirited, the actor is bound to 'jump up and down' and be constantly in motion. In fact it could just as readily be the complete opposite.

From the exercises they gradually move into rehearsing the second act. Getting as far as Shamraev's entrance, the rehearsal breaks off, and K.S. suggests he deal only with Tarasova, [Mikhail] Chekhov, and Khokhlov.

The whole rehearsal ends with an analysis of Nina's first line after Trigorin's exit, when she is alone: 'How strange this is, a famous writer . . .' etc.

14 September 1917

Individual work with Tarasova, [Mikhail] Chekhov and Trigorin [Khokhlov]. Act II.

They start by going over the first act.

What is the best way to clarify Nina's attitude to Treplyov and Trigorin?

It has to be broken down into small segments.

Once the segments become clearly understood, one has to 'model' segment by segment. And this will clarify the attitude. And to 'model' a segment accurately, one has to know the precise problem in the segment.

Let's take the biggest segment in the first act – Treplyov's meeting with Nina. The closest through-action for Nina is to act on stage, to be a success, etc. Connected with this through-action at the very beginning, Nina wants to know the truth: is she late or not? Which means, there's a moment of enquiry, she is seeking, she wants to find out whether it's all over or not. You have to experience the 'physical truth' of the enquiry. After: 'Of course, you're not late' – she is convinced. To reinforce this, you have to fit the keys to this scene: arriving, looking around, calming down – relaxing.

These keys may change over the course of the work. It's the internal modelling of the segment.

(Next segment.) Treplyov: 'No, no!'

Which is more important for Treplyov at that moment – his play or Nina?

Nina, because he loves her. She has destroyed his mental equilibrium.

What is the nature of this feeling of love? 'The key?' 'You hear her footsteps?' – 'Even the sound of her footsteps is pleasant!' The greater the love, the greater the attention. The greater the attention, the fewer smiles. Maybe a smile may come, but a mile of strained attention, tension. He wants to share his attention with his uncle. To infect him, to persuade him of his feelings.

Keys [Treplyov]: (1) to listen to the footsteps, (2) to infect his uncle with his attention, to persuade him.

You have to find the salient word for this, to come to love it. This word cannot be found with the mind – it turns things cold, but you will find this word, and come to love it from frequent repetition.

She arrives. The nature of his feeling, *the key – to welcome her* (to express to her all his sensations, his joy).

Now the next phase.

When you want to tell someone something important, you don't begin by saying it, yet you don't calm down, you don't relax after fatigue. Which means, for Nina it's *preparation*, to say something important, to prepare the ground.

To depict one's inner feeling, one has to draw a whole series of little pictures, in order to achieve the overall big picture. What kind of feeling leads to 'There are tears in your little eyes'? It's all offensive, annoying, inauthentic. Which means, the picture will be painted with a feeling of offence, annoyance, inauthenticity.

In an exercise Tarasova tries out Nina's first entrance, using K.S.'s directions, his 'keys'. The experiment is a *wonderful* success.

At this point Treplyov needs not a smile, but high spirits, great energy, activity. This is the sequence: activity, hence energy, high spirits, and high spirits may even lead to a smile.

In the next segment the salient word to choose is 'father': '*Father* knows nothing [about her leaving home].' This is not emphasis, but choice.

One must remember the 'given circumstances': 'What will happen to her if she doesn't get home in half an hour?' The circumstance is very important, and the colours must be laid on thick.

To convince people one needs calm, not electrical shocks, pressure.

One has to play psychological turning-points the way Duse, Kommissarzhevskaia [did].

For Treplyov 'the given circumstances' are also important: they are: in order for the play to go on, it will be illustrated by a word: where is this salient word?

Hence Treplyov's great activity, his desire to act quickly.

Nina is confused.

The love scene does not occur by chance. At any other time Nina would probably never say such a thing ['My heart is full of you']. She is afraid of the feeling of love and [love for] the stage. Thanks to their activity a love scene evolved. Love in Nina would come somewhat unconsciously.

You have to determine the exact way to solve all these problems in Nina: all joyously, all fearfully, all youthfully, which means, all expansively, rapidly. So you can weep as easily as you burst into laughter unconfined.

You have to lay a general colour over all the problems.

'Father and stepmother won't allow me. . . .' The key: she is *drawn* here. In the words: 'My heart is full of you' – she shows how she's drawn here. What she sees in him is art, Bohemia, but *not himself*.

The kiss is accidental, 'stupid'. He goes first. He is enthralled, absurd. People act foolishly at moments like this. They've lost their heads. Hence her question: 'What kind of tree is that?' His 'lecture' about how evening darkens all objects – that's also the result of awkwardness.

Their fright at Yakov's voice.

Would it be interesting, artistic, if all sincere, authentic feelings were *honestly* put on stage? *No.* You have [to add] a certain amount of acting, that is, a loving enjoyment of the role, of *acting the role*, but *acting the role* is not true stage art. All our psycho-physical work is necessary to mastering a role so that one can play the role and lovingly have fun with it.

Whenever the mind has gone through the psycho-physical process in a role, one can begin to enjoy the role, to play it.

Nina does not believe in [Trigorin] Treplyov as a writer. She doesn't understand him.

Again 'they play the whole scene.' K. S. says that [Treplyov] does not have to touch Nina. No physical intimacy. It's as if in the first scene [of Nina and Treplyov] there is no joyousness, merriment, hope, high spirits. . . . They have to ascend to heaven, so that [Treplyov's] fall in the second act will be tragic. Her excitement, fear, worship of Trigorin make sense of the second act. One has to select salient words for this: 'Trigorin', 'a famous writer,' 'it's dreadful for Mama (Arkadina)', and it goes without saying it's all about Trigorin.

Then K. S. makes a few remarks about Treplyov and Trigorin.

17 September 1917

Analysis of Act III. The scene of Treplyov and his mother.

Grounds for reconciliation with his mother are found, and only Trigorin, their type of theatre divides them again. And at the end of the quarrel he, Treplyov, immediately loses self-control, consciousness. The breaking point began with Trigorin; in the lines about theatre Treplyov is defending all art. 'Decadent' is the complete break.

'Skinflint!' The end of the anger, the culminating point. After this scene an enormous pause.

The nature of Arkadina's feelings here are all depicted through frivolity (with Sorin).

Arkadina is very stingy.

Sorin's request [that she give] money for Kostya's trip abroad puts Arkadina in a panic.

You have to validate this feeling by an example from life: at first there will be a moment of intense attention, 'probing' the heart of the person making the request. Self-defence. 'My costumes alone . . .' is at first a way of protecting herself from the 'trip abroad'. And then when she sees that the request is not especially insistent, she drops the costumes. The salient word in this scene is *'all the same'*. When this word is to be played, you must find for yourself further on.

You mustn't confuse the problem with the way in which the problem will be resolved.

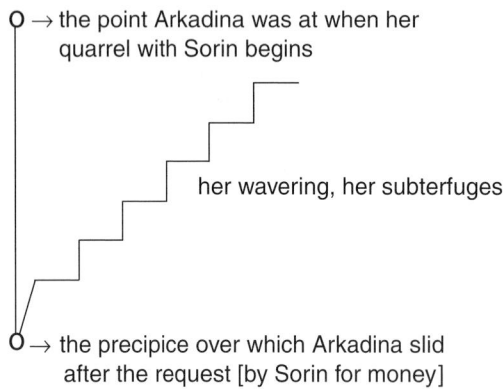

→ the point Arkadina was at when her quarrel with Sorin begins

her wavering, her subterfuges

→ the precipice over which Arkadina slid after the request [by Sorin for money]

There is a great moment of entreaty in the scene. The stingier she is, the greater the entreaty. She turns pale with horror. Therefore, when Kostya asks on Sorin's behalf, without knowing that Sorin had already asked on his behalf, she falls

into even greater horror, and Kostya's request for a bandage is a request to change the subject, and she does so joyfully, for her it's a bridge for crossing over to another theme.

'You won't do any more click-click?' – 'No, Mama, it won't happen again.'

Here there is a certain fear of committing suicide. He is examining his feelings. To understand him properly, you must find the salient word, the key. 'That was a moment *of insane despair*, when I could not get control of myself. It won't happen again.' Analyzing himself, Kostya persuades himself not to do it again.

The key is auto-suggestion.

Pause. He kisses her hand. This connects with the auto-suggestion. That kiss connects him physically with life. It is a straw he grasps at. Hence the tenderness to his mother.

Kostya's memories of his mother's kindness are important in characterizing Arkadina. She does not remember her own kind deeds, but she does remember the ballerinas, who drank coffee at her place. His memories provide him some foundation for a future life.

What's the reason he remembers: does he actually recall it or is he painting a picture of a blissful life? He is *painting,* because the pictures of a blissful life connect him with life, hence the salient words: '*golden hands*', 'you remember', 'how can you not remember', 'these last few days, these days I love you as tenderly and uninhibitedly as in childhood'. Pause. This line consolidates the relationship.

When he goes on to mention Trigorin, he speaks very carefully, at first continuing to consolidate the relationship. If the whole previous dialogue was a mutual desire for peace and quiet, based on certain compromises, her line 'I respect that man' will be very restrained, and the whole scene will be restrained. And the more restrained, the more powerful and tense it is, and if there's an outburst, it will be a real one.

The scene has to accumulate. Both of them plead not to destroy the relationship that's going so well. A compromise isn't found.

'Go back to your darling theatre . . . ' – he has exploded once and for all.

'I am more talented than the lot of you . . . ' is very modest, but convinced.

If this whole little scene contains three huge psychological 'phases', so that everything is exhausted, the pause will be huge.

Phases:

(1) You have to calm yourself physically (he walks around, he calms down).

(2) He understands, he appreciates what is happening.

(3) Isolation.

This is only a hint. The actor's personal temperament can alter this logical division of a pause into phases.

So it is with Arkadina:

(1) She calms down.

(2) She justifies herself ('Nonentity'), has understood.

(3) Watches furtively, imperceptibly gropes for his situation.

(4) Asks forgiveness; contrition.

'If you only knew: I've lost all hope.'

Again a straw, but not because he loves her again, he's simply holding on to her physically. Here again he is in the despair of the second act. Activity, seeking a way out, for otherwise the actor will play despair.

Here: 'Save me! Help!'

A scene of reconciliation. She pleads with all her blandishments for forgiveness, while he, burrowing into his soul, can hardly find a reason to embrace her again. He seeks support, he wants to be understood. And his embrace comes not from love, but from entreaty. She senses his condition and wants to help him.

The next segment: 'We're reconciled now?' – 'Yes, Mama.'

K.S. suggests going on stage and physically verifying the truth. Knipper and [Mikhail] Chekhov play an exercise from the scene.

Clichés prevailed, especially in [Mikhail] Chekhov, where he wants to show his affection, love for his mother. Both make many automatic emphases.

It works best without words – finding the physical truth.

Moreover one must live according to the ultimate problems (actions), and not by moving from problem to problem.

One must think not about how to do something, but what to do. Then something integral will result, physical truth will be freshly minted.

K. S. plays an exercise – the search for a lost pin.

In all the twists and turns of the acting one must sense that one exists: *I am.*

19 September 1917

Owing to Tarasova's illness the rehearsal takes on the character of a lecture. K. S. talks a lot about Nina in Acts II and III.

Translation © L. P. Senelick 2004

Notes and References

1. A vivid depiction of Moscow and the Art Theatre at this period appears in Richard Boleslavski and Helen Woodward, *Lances Down: Between the Fires in Moscow* (Indianapolis: Bobbs-Merrill, 1932).

2. There is a legend that when Richard Boleslavski taught Stanislavsky's ideas at the American Laboratory Theatre in the 1920s, his Polish accent pronounced 'beads' as 'beats', hence the common practice of breaking a scene down into 'beats'. Another version has Maria Ouspenskaya's Russian accent mispronouncing 'bits' to the same effect.

3. From I. N. Vinogradskaya, ed., *Stanislavskii repetiruet. Zapisi i stenogrammy repetitsy* [*Stanislavsky Rehearses: Rehearsal Notes and Transcripts*], 2nd ed. (Moscow: Moskovsky Khudozhestvenny teatr, 2002).

4. Mchedelov served as one of the assistant directors on the production.

5. A charity performance of Nemirovich-Danchenko's *The Lucky Devil* with the participation of the Maly actors took place on 27 March 1892. Stanislavsky played the artist Bogucharov and the excellent actress Glikeriya Fedotova his wife.

6. The leitmotiv of the heroines of *Three Sisters*.

7. In the First Studio's production of *Wandering Minstrels* by V. M. Vol'kenshtein (1914), Baksheev played the boyar Yavolod.

8. Mariya Savina (1854–1915), imperious prima donna of the Alexandra Theatre in St Petersburg; no great admirer of Chekhov, she played Arkadina a couple of times in 1902.

9. A reference to the scene 'The Kingdom of the Future' in Maeterlinck's *Blue Bird*, where the boy and girl Tyltyl and Mytyl are guided by the Soul of the World into the realm of the unborn.

John Stokes

'Lion Griefs': the Wild Animal Act as Theatre

This essay is concerned with the history of wild animal training between the early nineteenth and the mid-twentieth centuries, specifically with circus acts involving 'big cats'. The author, John Stokes, is sympathetic to the view that such performances are inhumane, degrading to animal and human alike, but rather than simply rehearsing familiar attitudes, he subjects the 'big cat' act to a performance analysis based on established criteria, in the belief that, if performance theory is to have the widespread application that its advocates claim, then it should be able to elucidate many different kinds of theatrical event. His primary materials are the myriad biographies and autobiographies of wild animal trainers that were produced during the heyday of their art, and which he finds to be frequently characterized by an unexpected thoughtfulness and breadth of experience, besides being highly informative about performance aesthetics. John Stokes is Professor of Modern British Literature in the Department of English, King's College London. He is a regular theatre reviewer for the *Times Literary Supplement* and co-author, together with Michael R. Booth and Susan Bassnett, of *Bernhardt, Terry, Duse: the Actress in Her Time* (Cambridge, 1988) and *Three Tragic Actresses* (Cambridge, 1996).

That later we, though parted then,
May still recall these evenings when
Fear gave his watch no look;
The lion griefs loped from the shade
And on our knees their muzzles laid,
And Death put down his book.

W. H. Auden,
'Out on the Lawn I Lie in Bed'

'The sign has come,' said Zarathustra, and his heart was transformed. And in truth, when it grew clear before him, there lay at his feet a sallow, powerful animal that lovingly pressed its head against his knee and would not leave him, behaving like a dog that has found his old master again. The doves, however, were no less eager than the lion with their love; and every time a dove glided across the lion's nose, the lion shook its head and wondered and laughed.

Friedrich Nietzsche,
Thus Spake Zarathustra

THE HISTORY of the circus can be told in many ways. Its origins can be located in English menageries as well as in Roman arenas; it can be seen as inherently cosmopolitan, based upon itinerant families rather than indigenous race; and yet it is associated with national ways of life – those proud Parisian amphitheatres built at the height of the Second Empire, the all-American bombast of the great travelling shows of Barnum and Bailey's and the Ringling Bros. The circus is pastoral: the cult of the small English tenting troupe as it moves through a green and pleasant land, so charmingly evident in the art of Edward Seago and Laura Knight. But it is urban as well: the annual ritual of Bertram Mills's Christmas season at Olympia, attended by generals, prime ministers, and royalty, was a feature of London life for several decades.

These powerful associations should not conceal the fact that many of the supposedly 'traditional' acts changed quite rapidly. In fact, the better circus histories – they are usually written by extremely well-informed *aficionados* – make a great deal of this dimension.[1] They tell, for instance, of how the heyday of the wild animal act lasted for less than two centuries and how it triumphed along with other contemporary designations of man's relationship with 'the natural'. When Joseph Goebbels and Hermann Goering saw a French trainer in Berlin just before the Second World War, Goebbels was heard to comment that his act was too brutal: 'German trainers perform much more gently. It's probably a ques-

 NTQ 20:2 (MAY 2004) © CAMBRIDGE UNIVERSITY PRESS DOI: 10.1017/S0266464X04000041

tion of race and atavism.' In response to the Frenchman's explanation that, unlike the German trainers, this one was working with a mixed group of various species, a quite different situation, Goebbels is said to have replied, 'That's the real solution! A single race is always preferable! Look at us – we have only one race: the German.'[2]

To the arts of performance, however contrived, we all bring our political ideologies to bear. It was at much the same inter-war moment that a circus historian described how observing a mixed group of lions and tigers, polar bears, and brown bears made her think of the League of Nations: 'All is peace so long as the trainer is there to keep order, but if he trips chaos results and the blood flows.'[3]

This essay traces the rise and fall of one branch of the animal act from its emergence in the early nineteenth century, when it first established itself as part of the entertainment scene, to its recent but still incomplete demise. It does so by considering the acts primarily as theatre. There are many good reasons for discontinuing the use of wild (and even domestic) animals for our amusement,[4] but I want to consider the case in terms of performance alone, partly as a contribution to the current concern with the relation between human and non-human,[5] but primarily in order to reinforce the claims of its advocates that performance theory is able to elucidate many different kinds of theatrical event.[6]

Origins of Modern Lion Taming

Happily, it is no longer easy, in the United Kingdom at any rate, to witness wild animal acts, and, as with all live performances, the immediacy of past events is lost for ever. But the records remain: reviews, paintings, photographs, histories – and pre-eminently the biographies and autobiographies of the trainers themselves. These invariably include statements of intention, descriptions of dramatic effect whether desired or achieved, aesthetic manifestos, and pleas of self-justification. Whether written alone or in collaboration, the lives of the trainers comprise a surprisingly serious and often rather well-written body of work that deserves to be read on its own terms, as a record of expertise and of vocation. That we will sometime discover the contradictions, evasions, and downright dishonesty common to autobiography proves little in itself; the trainers had special talents, their lives were demanding, their ideals complex. And they reached huge audiences.

I have further confined myself to discussions of acts involving the 'big cats', primarily lions and tigers, on the grounds that the trainers – though they may have worked on occasion with elephants, say, or with bears – did tend to specialize, and all insisted upon the deep psychological differences between species. Of all wild creatures, lions are the most mythologized – from Daniel, Androcles, and Saint Anselm through to Disney's epic for stage and screen, *The Lion King*. As the author of *Wild Animals in Captivity* announced in 1898:

So much has been written and said in praise of this powerful brute, of his noble disposition and his respect and forbearance towards mankind, that many persons are deluded into a belief that a lion is less to be feared than any of the other large carnivora, and one of the most telling exhibitions that have from time to time appeared before the public consists of performing lions and their tamers.[7]

However, most conventional accounts of modern lion trainers begin with one man: an American named Isaac Van Amburgh, who began by travelling as a wild animal dealer in the early nineteenth century. Van Amburgh made his debut as a trainer in New York in 1833 and five years later, hired by the celebrated equestrian Andrew Ducrow, made his first London appearance at Astley's, where he was said to have earned the very considerable sum of £300 a week. Later he transferred to Drury Lane, where Queen Victoria went to see him at least six times – including his appearance with his lions and tigers in the pantomime of *Harlequin Jack Frost* in 1839.

Involvement within a dramatic narrative was certainly within Van Amburgh's capabilities (in 1848 he returned to Astley's to play in *Morok the Beast Tamer*, based on Eugène Sue's *The Wandering Jew*), but his basic act simply required him to demonstrate his power over his animals with the use of whips and pistol shots, and then to reveal a unique personal rapport by mingling among them unharmed. A contemporary American admirer explains these apparently contradictory activities:

Mr Van Amburgh is a very religious man, and the notion of taming these savage creatures first came into his head from reading a passage in the first chapter of Genesis, while he was a boy. He was there told that to man had been given dominion over every thing that moved upon the earth; so that afterwards, whenever he heard of a man flying from a tiger, or having been devoured by a lion, he said to himself, 'This ought not to be: it was the man's fault!'[8]

Van Amburgh was twice painted by Sir Edwin Landseer, the most fashionable painter of the day. The first picture, 'Van Amburgh and His Animals', which was commissioned by Queen Victoria and delivered in 1839, is still in the Royal Collection. This shows the tamer surrounded by his big cats while a lamb leans against his breast. Victoria thought it 'quite beautiful, like nature', and she noted, quite correctly, that 'you are supposed to be inside the cage'.

The other painting was commissioned by the Duke of Wellington probably at the same time, but it was not ready until 1847. Entitled 'Portrait of Mr Van Amburgh, as He Appeared with his Animals at the London Theatres', it shows Van Amburgh holding a far more commanding stance which, as a note on the frame attests, is clearly supposed to emblematize Genesis. The second painting is a rather more complicated image than one might suppose, with all manner of symbolic references and echoes of other paintings by other artists;[9] it has even been suggested that it has a satirical aim, intended to cut Van Amburgh down to size. But the fact remains that together the two pictures are highly suggestive of the ways in which wild animal acts can be made to serve the intellectual and emotional needs of spectators. Needless to say, they tell us little about the needs of the animals themselves, unless we take those to be somehow expressed in postures of submission, resentful or acceptive.

Not Just Taming but Training

Van Amburgh died of a heart attack in Philadelphia in 1865; but already during his lifetime, along with trainers working in his tradition, there were others who were beginning to modify the familiar act so that the emphasis would begin to fall upon 'training' and upon the teaching of tricks rather than on simple 'taming'. Nevertheless, this process was quite gradual. Mid-Victorian spectators were said to be disappointed by the lions of another American trainer, John Carter, whose animals (they included horses, zebras, ostriches, and crocodiles) seemed in comparison with Van Amburgh's troupe to lack ferocity.[10] And as late as the 1930s Edward Seago could still record seeing a travelling circus that advertised in big blue-and-yellow letters 'A Lion Hunt! A Lion Fight!' with underneath in red, 'The Big Cage in Reality!', and the promise to view inside 'The Lion Who Killed His Trainer!'[11]

The most significant English animal trainer at the turn of the century was probably Frank Bostock, though he later spent a good deal of time in America. Bostock was descended from the family of George Wombwell, who had established an early English animal collection in 1805; by the mid-nineteenth century 'Bostock and Wombwell' was among the largest travelling shows of wild animals in England. Frank's father was himself an animal trainer and exhibitor, but his son, 'The Animal King', was to take the practice and the theory of training in much more ambitious and seemingly humane directions. In *The Training of Wild Animals* (1903) Bostock surveys and evaluates his contemporaries, always claiming to be kind in his methods, forgoing the use of pistols in the ring, and insisting that wild animals should never be punished for their misdemeanours.

Trainers traditionally distinguish two kinds of performance: '*en ferocité*', the kind of act associated with Van Amburgh, in which the trainer demonstrates dominance over his animals (from which it follows that they must initially show some signs of aggression), and '*en douceur*' or '*en pelotage*': those quieter acts in which an apparent docility

The two Landseer oil paintings of Van Amburgh. Above: 'Isaac Van Amburgh and His Animals' (The Royal Collection © 2004, Her Majesty Queen Elizabeth II). Below: 'Van Amburgh as He Appeared with His Animals at the London Theatre, 1847' (Yale Center for British Art, Paul Mellon Collection, USA: www.bridgeman.co.uk).

allows the trainer to put his charges through their paces. Although Bostock favoured training over taming, he remains a transitional figure, standing between the heroic figures of the nineteenth century and the more thought-ful if still glamorous stars of the twentieth. In the course of this initial survey I shall be introducing several of these later trainers, all of whose feats are now commemorated in circus literature. They include Captain Bonavita, a protégé of Bostock, who worked in America and who conducted himself in the ring with military bearing, insisting with steely bravado that 'A man does not refuse to go into battle because he has been hurt.'[12] (Bonavita lost an arm when he was attacked by a lion and eventually died as the result of being mangled by a bear.)[13]

Then there are several closely linked continentals. Julius Seeth, although German, started performing in St Petersburg in 1881, and became the owner of the largest troupe of his day, about twenty-five animals. (By the end of the First World War, a rival, 'Captain' Alfred Schneider, was appearing at Olympia with some fifty lions.)[14] Seeth, 'a fine figure of a man, six feet tall and broad in proportion with large moustache',[15] first visited London in 1887 and was still working at the London Hippodrome in 1906. So impressed was he by Seeth's act that Emperor Memlik III of Abyssinia presented him with a group of magnificent local lions.[16]

Richard Sawade, another German, famous for his modesty, toured the world with his tiger act for thirty years until he retired in 1919 at the age of fifty-two to concentrate solely on training;[17] while Rudolf Matthies, Sawade's pupil, said to be a man of almost saintly temperament with the 'kindliest of natures', was 'transmitted to the most ferocious of brutes on earth by that subtle radiation which only animal men know'.[18]

Among the Europeans who worked internationally somewhat later, in the mid-twentieth century, the greatest was widely held to be 'a stocky, rather diminutive Frenchman named Alfred Court'. When Court performed with Ringling-Barnum in 1940 he brought into the ring at one and the same time jaguars, leopards, panthers, and lions.[19] According to one admirer,

The most genial and personable of companions, suave and elegant outside the Big Cage, and possessed of a subtle sense of humour, Court belies the popular conception of the bold demigod, cruel and stern, who bends jungle kings to their duty by an overpowering personality and a bitter goad.[20]

In contrast, contemporary with Court, a particular favourite among English audiences,

was Togare, 'he-man of the circus world'.[21] Born in Serbia of a Turkish peasant mother, Togare started working with lions in Russia but ended up with Mills.[22] Their star trainer in the 1950s was more local – Alex Kerr, a Glaswegian who started off by working as a fairground hand before joining Mills in 1949.[23]

The Mills and the Chipperfields

Most of the major acts worked for Bertram Mills, although there were exceptions. One of these was the American Clyde Beatty, whose methods were disapproved of by some of the English trainers, even though he had in the 1950s perhaps the most sensational act in the world, so spectacular that it couldn't go on tour with Ringling Brothers but was mainly featured only when the circus played Madison Square Garden.[24] Beatty reintroduced that element of heroic machismo long ago associated with Van Amburgh. Not surprisingly perhaps, he was admired by Ernest Hemingway, who presented him with a copy of *Death in the Afternoon*, his book on bull-fighting, and compared him to the great boxers of the day, Gene Tunney and Jack Dempsey.[25]

Neither did the most renowned female trainer of the age appear at Olympia. This was Mabel Stark, best known for her tigers, especially a fine Bengal male named Rajah who had been raised as a pet and with whom she developed a remarkable routine, but also for her mixed groups which included panthers. Stark remained charismatic even in her old age and gave training classes to young women who aspired to become like her.[26] Mills did have female trainers none the less, among them, in the 1930s, Priscilla Kayes, who apparently gave 'the impression of respecting the moods and wiles of her lions, but at the same time of showing no fear'.[27]

Although the Mills family dominated in modern times, the most celebrated – and on occasion notorious – English circus dynasty is that of the Chipperfields, who can trace their ancestry back to the winter of 1684 when an ancestor took a performing bear onto the ice of the frozen Thames.[28] Since that time the Chipperfields have intermarried with other circus families and have been continuously involved with animals. In the mid-nineteenth century they added wirewalkers, acrobats, and clowns to their travelling menagerie, and became more of a circus proper, a tradition furthered by the work of James (born in 1824) and Richard (1874–1959). In more recent times, Dick Chipperfield (born in 1904), his brother Jimmy Chipperfield

Opposite page, top: Alfred Court with Maouzi. Opposite page, bottom: Togare: 'the he-man of the circus world'. Left: Clyde Beatty in action

(born in 1912), and Jimmy's daughter Mary (born in 1938) have all written autobiographies in which animals play an important part.

Qualities of a Satisfying Show

As even this opening summary suggests, certain differences in approach are clearly visible between generations and, to a lesser extent, between nationalities, but, following the usual practice of theatrical analysis, I'll begin my commentary proper by identifying those qualities which have been most commonly said to contribute to the aesthetic coherence that makes for a satisfying show. Judging by the memoirs of both performers and spectators, there appear to be two main elements, and, curiously, they seem, at least on the surface, to be opposed to each other.

The first is 'flow', as used in Alex Kerr's insistence that 'it should all be flow – from one animal to another, from one trick to another – building up to a climax that comes right at the end',[29] or, as another trainer puts it, the need is that 'the act will flow smoothly' because 'an act is like a watch. The tricks have to fit into each other as neatly as cogs and flywheels.'[30] The other key element is 'risk' which, although not named as often as 'flow', is obviously present in the continual descriptions of what is physically at stake in a wild animal act and, of course, in the imperative to provide an audience with excitement.

Clearly there is a theatrical tension between the smooth, unimpeded interaction of man and beast and the ever-present threat of violent disruption. If there were any doubt about the dangerous nature of these acts, it is answered by the strange pride that trainers take in displaying their wounds, even vicariously through the text to their readers. There is an anecdote about Mabel Stark that tells how one of the young women who admired her so much once asked her what it took to be a trainer. Slowly Stark pushed her legs from under her dressing gown. 'This,' she said. From her feet to her thighs she was covered with scars.[31]

Like the gashes proudly displayed by chivalric knights – like stigmata even – wounds are visible testimonies of an honourable sacrifice ostensibly made for the sake of an audience, but equally endured by the trainers on behalf of their own vocation. Although the trainers are in some ways only subject to the same conditions as other circus artists – the need to balance flow against risk is shared with acrobats, trapeze artists, and so on – the wild animal acts combine the two in a unique way, since without risk there might, at least in the early days, have been very little left to hold the attention. The stress on wounds is quite exceptional. It points to a peculiar sense of initiation, a fellowship among trainers, and, even more importantly, of intimacy with the animal who has caused the damage.

Yet the animal act is no ritual where some religious or ethnic qualification might be required before participation. Nor is it (though the comparison is sometimes made) like a bull-fight, where death is the desired end, but simply part of an entertainment that traditionally claims to bring pleasure to everyone, young and old, irrespective of background. Its desired effect, then, is that of a complex whole, depending upon a combination of proximity and distance, a mixture of dominance and vulnerability, of harmonious certainty and the ever-present risk. This effect can only be achieved by theatrical means, including scenography and the creation of a suitable performance space that makes no attempt at illusion but allows rather for a three-dimensional perception of contained actuality.[32]

Setting, Props, and Costumes

The 'big cage' of the animal act is now so familiar that we may not realize that it is of relatively recent design. In fact, it seems to have been introduced in the late nineteenth century in place of the travelling cage (which is where trainers had traditionally worked) by the German trainer Carl Hagenbeck, probably the most influential figure in the whole history of wild animal training. Hagenbeck, whose family were animal dealers as well as pioneers in new ways of presenting animals in zoos 'without bars', realized that a circular cage that fitted neatly within the ring would enable the wild animal acts to become a more integral part of the circus bill.[33]

The idea caught on, and brought with it several new developments. The size of the big cage invited ever more ambitious acts featuring a greater number of animals. Even so, the time-consuming complexity of setting it up meant that animal acts tended to open the show. If the act was positioned in the middle of the circus bill, then the period of construction had to be covered by clowns, or perhaps by a speech from the ringmaster, who, in the early days of the big cage at any rate, would explain to the audience the riskiness of what was about to take place.

At the same time as the big cage frames the performance, so it contains and changes spatial relationships. We will obviously think of the space between the spectator and the animals, but we should also consider the spaces within the cage, specifically between human and animal and between the animals themselves. The round cage provides no corners into which an animal might retreat in order to defend itself. This is important in terms of the kind of effect being sought. So, for instance, with an old-fashioned violent act in which the animal is actually required to show signs of aggression, then the trainer might deliberately violate its personal area – the 'flight distance' or space that it needs for any escape – in order to provoke a violent response.

In the case of a more modern kind of act, in which the trainer wishes to demonstrate his ease and familiarity with his animals, then they will need to have been trained to allow him to come up close. Some say that this kind of intimate spatial relationship is actually more dangerous because the animal might at any point forget what it knows and react to the slightest disturbance by lashing out at any nearby human.[34] Dick Chipperfield explains it like this:

In one way a lion is very like a human: he does not like anyone to come too close to him. Just as most people prefer to keep a slight distance between themselves and their fellows, and feel pressured if bores at cocktail parties lean closer and closer, thrusting right into their faces to talk, so lions need a certain minimum distance between themselves and their handler – and this built-in repulsion factor is the cornerstone of most training.[35]

Props also play their part in the orchestration of space, and more generally. The most important is the stick or whip that gives direction and acts as an impregnable extension of the trainer's body. In the early days of animal acts after Van Amburgh, use of the whip might have been augmented with pistol shots but these became less common with changes in the approach to training and for very many years trainers have insisted that the whip is never used to inflict pain.

If we are to believe the great majority of them, it is non-functional – or rather, its function is only partially what it appears to be, that of a weapon, and much more that of a pointer, an indicator of direction and occasionally, perhaps, a curb. Semiotically, it is an object divested of its primary significance in order to take on a secondary role, but it is hard to believe that an audience, unversed in animal training, would necessarily appreciate that shift – or that a trainer would easily refrain from exploiting the ambiguity. Alfred Court hints at something more sinister when he asserts that, 'In fact, the stick and the whip are as necessary as the reward of meat, the soft voice and the caresses.'[36]

Props obviously connect with costume and, once again, we find a great deal of historical variation. Judging by Landseer, Van Amburgh affected a gladiatorial breast-plate and occasional toga. Bostock liked a kind of keeper's outfit; Captain Bonavita assumed a military-style uniform as befitted his (fictitious) rank. George Conklin, who worked in America from the 1860s, 'dressed in elaborate Roman tights covered with spangles, and across the top of the cage was painted in great letters, "Conklin is Our Master".'[37]

Rudolf Matthies dressed himself up as an Indian rajah, with oriental robes of blue and gold and a white crested turban: 'His movements are slow and his calm manner full of dignity. Eleven tigers prowl around him and strike fantastic poses at his bidding.'[38] Togare wore a costume apparently modelled on Rudolph Valentino's in *The Sheik*[39] – 'bright-

Above: Priscilla Kayes at Bertram MIlls in the 1930s.
Right: practising the 'gentling' method of training.

coloured Turkish pantaloons, enormous brass ear-rings, a jet-black wig, and his face and body . . . painted mahogany colour'.[40]

Alex Kerr affected high riding boots and embroidered jodhpurs, while Priscilla Kayes, tempted fate in 'shiny black Wellingtons, white breeches and shirt, and flame-coloured silk scarf'.[41] In the 1970s there was at least one trainer working who went for a red vinyl Roman charioteer's outfit, while Gunther Gebel Williams, a very big star in his time, favoured long blond hair and spangles much like the glam-rock singers of the period.[42]

Costumes signify the authority that the trainer has conferred upon him- or herself and they anticipate and direct the audience's reading of their performance. And it is at this point that, following conventional perform-ance analysis, we might expect to go on to consider the input of the individuals them-selves. But, immediately, a fundamental issue presents itself. Who, in fact, is the performer in the animal act, the animal or the trainer? Indeed, can either or both really be said to 'perform' at all?

Paradoxes of the 'Gentling' Approach

At first glance it would seem unlikely that animals can ever 'perform' in one sense of the word, since they are normally held to be incapable of conscious deception. In fact pro-fessional opinions are mixed on this point, and often contradictory. The whole question is complicated by the fact that an historical break took place around the turn of the century. A new approach to training, parallel to that devised by Bostock but different in its detail, was introduced which, by changing the assumed relation between man and beast, affected ideas of animal participation. This was the so-called 'gentling' method, once again devised by Carl Hagenbeck in Hamburg in the late 1880s, whereby an animal was not to be asked to do anything that did not come 'naturally'.

In his autobiography, Carl Hagenbeck lays down a few very basic rules. Not only must animals be kindly treated on the model of pupil and teacher and be well rewarded, they must never be blamed or punished for any misdemeanour.[43] By building on instinct and

146

traits, eliminating or reducing the element of fear, Hagenbeck claimed that it would be possible to have an animal perform remarkable feats without undue cruelty or coercion. The trainer is always responsible.

'Gentling' is not merely a preparation for performance, it affects the very concept of performance itself because if it is true that the animal is now required to do only what it is physically and psychically inclined to do, then movements in the ring and their relation to the trainer will change accordingly. For years the Hagenbecks supplied circuses with previously trained animals, though this practice was looked down upon by those who insisted upon raising their own animals virtually from their birth.[44] And, of course, the extent to which Hagenbeck's principles were respected by others far away from Hamburg remains a very open question, although few modern trainers failed to pay lip-service to them.

It is certainly worth making the obvious but unanswerable point that Hagenbeck's methods, however widespread, by no means eradicated violence, contrived or otherwise. It is hard to see how such Hagenbeck tricks as a tiger riding on the back of a horse – two very different creatures brought into close proximity with one another – can be described as 'natural'. Given the circumstances in which the acts took place, fights between animals and attacks on trainers continued to be inevitable.

Some accounts stress the ways in which natural aggression can be built into the act to appear as something other than it is:

In nearly every wild animal act one of the beasts, generally a lion, refuses to go on with his part. He roars, snarls, crouches, and acts as if he were going to tear the trainer to pieces. The trainer, in turn, gives the impression that the whole thing has happened unexpectedly, and as a result the audience moves to the edge of its seat and begins biting its nails. With a great show of prod and whip the man at last conquers the king of beasts who, after all is said and done, is nothing but a stooge. Outside the big cage he is generally the most docile of all the cats. . . . Occasionally the wrong lion or tiger will get temperamental. He will act just like the stooge, and the trainer will have to prod him to force him into line. It looks to the spectators as if he is really hurting the animal, but

as a matter of fact he isn't. No sensible trainer will unnecessarily enrage one of his beasts and thereby risk a real fight in full view of his audience.[45]

In fact, the testimonies of the trainers vary so greatly that invocation of Hagenbeck's 'gentling' raises as many performative problems as it solves. Can a harsh command be given without a harsh effect? In other words, can a trainer disguise, 'perform', his own role? If so, might not that work in either of two ways: with either a trainer pretending to be authoritarian in order to exaggerate the need to control the animals and to impress an audience with their own privileged presence; or, conversely, assuming nonchalance in order to demonstrate his mastery over a genuine danger?

Self-Presentation of the Performer

At the same time as the concept of animal performance underwent significant change as a result of 'gentling', so the self-presentation of the trainer shifted in the context of wider cultural assumptions. Around the turn of the century trainers sometimes liked to present themselves as Nietzscheans who were demonstrating their oneness with nature by matching its innate courage with a display of their own self-mastery. Thus Bostock in 1903:

The ideal animal trainer is a man of superb physique. His eyes are clear, his muscles hard and sinewy, his limbs well grown, his body well developed, and his clean, healthy skin shows the warm blood circulating beneath. He is without blemish physically and his mental capabilities are good. He knows men as well as animals. He makes a versatile application of that knowledge; he knows the traits, the history, and the tendencies of those animals which form his life study, and on the constant use of that knowledge depends his dominance.[46]

The superman is an inherently male concept, but female trainers also capitalized on gender types – Priscilla Kayes, for instance, who would occasionally admonish a lion 'with a lift of her finger, a truly typical feminine gesture'.[47] Some played against received ideas by taking them to extremes. Mabel Stark's most original invention was to turn her back on her favourite Rajah and have him leap on her as if in attack.[48] Having terrified her audience, Stark would then wrestle playfully with her pet before putting him through further tricks.

Racial types also played their part. In addition to the imperialistic white man in his pseudo-military uniform (Captain Bonavita and others), alone in an imaginary jungle, there were, for instance, the exotically bare-chested Togare and 'Damoo', a Hindu mystic, who 'although short of stature, often impresses his audiences as a giant' and who doubled for Tarzan in a film.[49]

If frames, props, and costumes are conventional components of most theatrical occasions, so too are the combined elements of disguise and personality, the expressive facade, that characterize public self-fashioning – and which become exceptionally problematic in the case of the wild animal acts. There remains a startling difference between these acts and all other forms of performative entertainment, from high-risk activities such as tight-rope walking to the most conventional forms of spoken drama. This is the almost complete absence of trust between participants – an absence so unique that it requires especially close attention.

The Element of Risk

Among the trainers there is absolute unanimity on the single point that no wild animal, however familiar, can be entirely relied upon. Here, for instance, is Bostock in 1903, drawing on an hierarchical or Darwinistic notion of what constitutes animal nature, its limited capacity for supposed development:

The only enemy feared by the larger wild beast is man. Why they should feel this supreme awe of man it is difficult to explain. Neither his size nor his erect position can account for it, and it is only in long and settled and much frequented regions that his firearms are dreaded. The explanation probably is that they are unable to comprehend his habits, to fathom his mental attitude, to learn what he is likely to do next, and are awed by the mystery of his conduct, as we might be by that of some supernatural being of unknown power who came among us and threatened our liberty and our happiness.

The minds of the great carnivora are little exercised in nature, and do not develop. Accustomed to seeing all the denizens of the forest quail before them, they do not know what it is to feel a sense of help needed or of favours granted. It is perfectly natural, then, that trainers should say that kindness is not appreciated by them. A tigress is, in most cases, as likely to eat up her keeper after six years of attention as she would be after six days.[50]

Actual experience tended to prove that his conclusion, if not his reasoning, was correct. Even Mabel Stark's beloved Rajah turned dangerous and unreliable in the end.[51] Clyde Beatty kept 'the animals sufficiently off-balance to prevent them from making a heavy spring for me'. Keeping them off-balance helped control 'the basic savagery that causes them to revert to type when you least expect it. . . . For as fond as I am of these rough, tough, wonderfully endowed play-mates of mine, I simply cannot afford to trust them fully.'[52]

But if trust – that cornerstone of group performance – is so noticeably absent in the trainer's relationship with his animals, what would ever make someone want to take up the job professionally? What are the personal requirements? The trainers offer different answers to that question. Thus Alfred Court:

To understand animals and to love them, to have endless patience, to be sober and capable of great physical endurance, and to possess a little courage – these, as I see it, are the qualities necessary to make one a trainer of cats.[53]

Court's close friend, a circus vet, testifies to a deeper and more exclusive explanation of Court's commitment to the animal world:

As we worked together, both to the same end, each of us realized – without either of us saying anything – that we were men who were happiest when we were working with animals. We weren't misanthropes: our relationships with people were excellent and enjoyable; but we were more at home with animals. When there had been a choice in our lives, each of us had always made the decision that kept us close to animals.[54]

Jim Frey, another successful trainer from the mid-twentieth century and a rather more philosophical Frenchman than his fellow-countryman Court, started out by questioning his own self-evident talents, asking himself if it was simply because the animals

Above: Alfred Court forces a tiger back to his stool.
Below: Jim Frey with a favourite tiger.

he dealt with were captive that he found them so easy to deal with. In the end he decided to go to Africa to test his power against animals in the wild. His experiences there were so inspiring that the very thought of returning to white 'civilization' filled him with depression:

Once again I should have to bow to those narrow laws that men have invented in the course of centuries to destroy their own happiness and stultify their own personalities. I could already hear the usual stupidities being talked about the ferocity of wild animals, the superiority of the white men to the black, and the superiority of intelligence to instinct. . . . Africa, the continent where man had interfered less with the natural harmony of forces than elsewhere, and where that baleful Cartesianism of which we are so foolishly proud has not altogether deadened the senses or distorted man's instinct. . . .[55]

Frey wonders if he will shock his readers when he says that he doesn't 'put them – or myself – one whit above the animals?' He confides:

When I hear people talking about 'our lower brethren' so very condescendingly, as though animals were inferior beings, it infuriates me. . . . I should like to know where the superiority of human beings is supposed to lie. Is it a self-evident superiority from a comparison of two modes of life? I hardly think so. It is true that we know a good many things animals don't know, but by the same token we are ignorant of a good many of the things they know. And our own moral standards are certainly less straightforward than theirs.[56]

Nevertheless, the professional performer for Frey is 'a man who has, by an effort of will, completely overcome his fear and always remains complete master of his reflexes and his actions. In other words, he has mastered himself before he attempts to master his animals. He demonstrates the superiority of man, which is something apart from his mortal envelope.'[57]

Clyde Beatty is somewhat less pretentious: 'It comes as a surprise to some that I love these animals and that the big cats and I have had a lot of fun together over the years.'[58] Alex Kerr betrays his own cultural moment when invoking a telepathic idea of

trainers, certainly when taken out of context, can sound remarkably similar to the beliefs professed by today's animal rights activists and environmental guardians. 'Just remember that we are all animals; we all belong to the same kingdom', writes the American author of *Lions 'n' Tigers "n' Everything* in the 1920s:

With that in mind, experiment with the idea of looking at those animals not as just so many mere brutes, but merely as a different branch of the animal kingdom to which you belong. Look upon them as foreigners, as visitors to your land from a different shore, strange but willing to learn, and with far greater perceptive powers, perhaps, than we have. [62]

The Viennese trainer Roman Proske believes that:

All the things I have been able to teach my jungle felines during a lifetime spent with them seem insignificant to me compared with the enlightenment I have derived from the animals themselves. I have always felt grateful to the Creator for the privilege of working with these truly majestic creatures, for they have never ceased to move me to wonder at their grace and beauty and imminent terror – a similar sense of awe and wonder, I think, that must have inspired William Blake when he wrote of their 'fearful symmetry'. [63]

For a few trainers, perhaps a minority, the ultimate proof that circus animals are not abused, that they are better off than they otherwise might be, is the visible pleasure they take in appearing before an audience. Bostock again:

Once thoroughly accustomed to the stage, they seem to find in it a sort of intoxication well known to a species higher on the order of nature. Nearly all trainers assert that animals are affected by the attitude of an audience, that they are stimulated by the applause of an enthusiastic house, and perform indifferently before a cold audience. [64]

Jimmy Chipperfield cites a trait apparently common to both wild and domestic animals: 'the desire to please: before long lions and tigers know perfectly well that they are part of an act, and they may become desperately keen to do their job well.' [65] One of Chipperfield's lions in particular, 'far from being the savage which she appeared to be,

mental communication. 'The easy, soft affection you give to a pet dog is not enough for wild cats', says Kerr. 'You need a deep love for them that comes from a complete understanding of their very different traits. But, most important of all, you must be able to sink your own personality and approach them on the level of their mentality.' This, apparently, 'is a very low level, far below, but something similar to, that of the primitive races: the Aborigines and the Pygmies.' [59]

Kerr's 'great ecstasies' come when he is practising with his animals:

They come from a sense of achievement when at last I have transmitted an idea from my mind into the mind of an animal without touching him; when, at last, all barriers are down and we completely understand and respect each other, without fear. [60]

Even Mary Chipperfield claims:

We are certainly not the last word in life. Man is no more important or essential than an elephant or an ant, a sparrow or an eagle. Most of them were here before us. Some may be here long after we have destroyed ourselves. . . . I learn all too little about life from people, but I learn something new every day from my animals, and so can everyone. [61]

Pleasure in Performance?

Holistically inclined, evidently respectful of the natural world, the testimonies of the

Opposite page: Alex Kerr with Khan. Above: Vojtek Trubka calls his 'cats' by name and they turn their faces towards him.

was a very complex character and played to the gallery as faithfully as a prima donna.'[66]

Even the philosophical Jim Frey insists that, 'Animals which are used to working in the circus-ring under full lighting, which allows them to see the audience quite clearly, are often upset when they have to work on a stage with footlights and limelights which blind them and rob them of the sight of their public.'[67] 'If a tiger was clever,' recalls Frey, 'he took a genuine delight in performing the tricks he was taught.' 'Animals were like human beings, there wasn't much difference between them! Inside the cage there was plotting, spite, and jealousy just as outside: the lion jealous of the tiger, the polar bear too indolent to share in the intrigues, but the other bears scheming against all in the cage', says another ringmaster.[68] One of Alex Kerr's old lions 'was a real artiste': 'He seemed to have timing, a feeling for effect. I had only to raise my stick to get a beautiful, seemingly realistic snarl out of him and yet the moment the cane was lowered he was quiet as a lamb.'[69]

Then again, in considerable contrast, the American George Keller, who later worked at Disneyland, insists that all cats are reluctant performers. 'Cats don't like to come out in the open, as they are forced to do in the big arena. They don't want to face their natural enemy, man. I think they sometimes perform with the thought in their minds that the sooner they get it over, the sooner they can get back to their cages.' Keller claims to have had only one animal that he thought really enjoyed working with him.[70]

No 'Return to Normality'

These testimonies are obviously very mixed. There is, however, one important respect in which the animal's conscious participation in an act, and hence perhaps its willingness, can be judged. The conclusion of any theatrical performance, at least in the West, is customarily marked by a bow from the performer and by applause from the audience: a formal and reciprocal recognition that a special event is over and that an enhanced normality is about to be resumed.

Although the trainers will indeed argue that lions and tigers respond to applause, they never suggest that their animals have anything like a full appreciation of what that might involve. After all, at the end of their show, the animals return to their cages alone and still feared. There is no reconciliation, no return home. This is a deep difference that helps to define the performative inadequacy of the wild animal act and seals its fate as a civilized theatrical entertainment. For domestic animals such as dogs or horses, the arena

151

of public performance extends to the off-stage world that they occupy alongside us; for wild animals the off-stage world – jungle, desert, savannah – has never been shared; and today, at a time of environmental crisis, it may even be lost for ever, leaving the animal quite literally with nowhere to go.

If we value theatre according to its capacity to involve, to entertain, to instruct, then wild animal acts score well in many respects. But they fail in others: absolute trust, mutuality between participants, the keystone of performance, is absent, as all the trainers admit, and there is no shared outside against which to set the inside of the show. Of course, the *illusion* of trust, the *illusion* of 'nature', may well be there but, even so, these bear no relation to our global experience, in which wild animals are on the decrease at the same time as the boundaries between human and non-human are being eroded by philosophers.

Although human performance obviously need not depend upon verbal language in order to communicate – we can enjoy plays in languages that we don't understand, we can appreciate mime and sports – we do always attribute freedom and intentionality to those involved, however distant and alien the immediate setting may be. This can never be the case with wild animals, whatever their trainers may sometimes claim. Yet we would be letting the trainers off too lightly if we simply left matters there. Who benefits from wild animal performance? Human performance is commonly held to be 'reflexive' in the sense that the individual 'reveals himself to himself', learning from the experience.[71]

The personal histories of the trainers suggest that this may indeed have been the case for some of them, but it is hard to believe that self-improvement was the case for their animals, since whatever they may have gained from performance (other than release from imposed boredom) was of no use either to themselves (as well as extending its abilities a domestic pet trained in obedience may lead a safer life) or, unlike a guide dog, to others. After all, even the supposedly humane principle of Hagenbeck's 'gentling' is based on the idea that you cannot teach an animal anything to which it is not *already* 'naturally inclined', which it does not, in some sense, already know. There can, in that very precise sense, be very little that is truly 'performative' in any display by a wild animal.

To look again at Landseer's highly theatrical painting for Queen Victoria of 'Van Amburgh and His Animals' is to realize that the real falsity of that representation lies not in the fact that the expressions of the wild animals are humanized but that, by acknowledging both the spectators and Van Amburgh himself, they are apparently benefiting from their situation. Consequently, it is perfectly safe to be in the cage with them, at least while Van Amburgh is in there too. Conversely, Wellington's commission shows the animals literally put in their place by theatrical means, by a mere, if authoritative, gesture. Both of Landseer's portraits of the trainer depend upon reciprocal relationships that have never been, and can never be, anything like so simple, so secure.

Animals are like us, but they are different too. In their daily routine the trainers lived with this troubling fact, although for whatever reasons – from commercial greed or necessity to genuine moral pride to a quasi-spiritual conviction – they sometimes could hardly bear to accept its truth, as the urgency and confusion of their autobiographies may tell us. And so they persisted in their art, hoping that, beyond the threat or promise of violence, the public might discover in the controlled animal act a vision of peaceful co-existence.

Not surprisingly, the motif of the lion and the lamb (an evocation of Isaiah, Chapter 11, Verse 6), which features in Landseer's paradise, is recurrent. The grandson of Lord George Sanger, a celebrated Victorian circus proprietor, tells how his relative had once been in conversation with a bishop who told him that peace on earth would only come about when the lion and the lamb should lie down side by side. Sanger at once went to work: 'A suitable lion cub was separated from the rest of the litter, a healthy lamb was purchased and placed in the same cage as the lion cub, and the two grew to maturity together.' Eventually Sanger was able to construct the 'Queen's tableau' which featured a live lion and a live lamb together with Britannia and a Life Guard. It represented, says the grandson an 'attempt to bring about the millennium'.[72]

That millennial tag is a very common one. 'Every animal trainer thoroughly understands what the public does not know', writes Bostock, 'that the trained animal is a product of science; but the tamed animal is a chimera of the optimistic imagination, a forecast of the millennium.'[73] Sometimes, quite often in fact, the trainers even managed to persuade themselves that the millennial vision was true. One Christmas Eve the Viennese trainer Roman Proske lay down with his tiger cubs listening to 'Silent Night'. 'Never had I known such complete happiness', he recalls, 'such a feeling of belonging. This was the peaceable kingdom of my dreams, when man and beast shall lie down together and possess their souls in God's love. Yes, as long as I live I shall never forget that perfect night before Christmas.'[74] It's a picture of undeniable beauty – and the deepest arrogance. The peaceable kingdom of the beasts is, as usual, a theatrical scene created by a man.

Notes and References

1. Circus studies are exceptionally well served by bibliographies. The most useful are the five volumes of R. Toole-Stott, *Circus and Allied Arts: a World Bibliography 1500–1957* (Derby: Harpur, 1958–92); and John M. Turner, *Victorian Arena: the Performers. A Dictionary of British Circus Biography*, two vols. (Formby, England: Lingdales Press, 1995 and 2000). I have found some of the best histories of the circus to be John S. Clarke, *Circus Parade* (London: Batsford, 1936); Antony Hippisley Coxe, *A Seat at the Circus* (London: Evans , 1951); Rupert Croft-Cooke and W. S. Meadmore, *The Sawdust Ring* (London: Odhams, 1951); Janet M. Davis, *The Circus Age: Culture and Society under the Big Top* (Chapel Hill; London, 2002); M. Willson Disher, *Greatest Show on Earth* (London: Bell, 1937); Paul Eipper, *Circus: Men, Beasts, and Joys of the Road*, trans. Frederick H. Martens (London: Routledge, 1931); Thomas Frost, *Circus Life and Circus Celebrities* (London: Tinsley Brothers, 1875); A. H. Kober, *Star Turns* (London: Noel Douglas, 1928); Rodney N. Manser, *Circus: the Development of the Circus, Past, Present, and Future* (Blackburn: Richford, 1987); Ruth Manning Sanders, *The English Circus* (London: Werner Laurie, 1952); George Speaight, *A History of the Circus* (London: Tantivy Press, 1980); Henry Thétard, *Coulisses et secrets du cirque* (Paris: Librarie Plon, 1934), and *La Merveilleuse Histoire du Cirque*, two vols. (Paris: Prisma, 1947).

2. Alfred Court, *Wild Circus Animals* (London: Burke, 1954), p. 148.

3. Bertha Bennet Burleigh, *Circus* (London: Collins, 1937), unpaginated.

4. The best presentation of arguments against the use of animals in circuses is William Johnson, *The Rose-Tinted Menagerie* (London: Heretic Books, 1990). Also see Charles R. Magel, *Keyguide to Information Sources in Animal Rights* (London: Mansell, 1989).

5. The touchstone here is Donna J. Haraway's much-quoted assertion: 'By the late twentieth century in United States scientific culture, the boundary between human and animal is thoroughly breached. The last beachheads of uniqueness have been polluted if not turned into amusement parks – language, tool use, social behaviour, mental events, nothing really convincingly settles the separation of human and animal.' See her *Simians, Cyborgs, and Women: the Reinvention of Nature* (London: Free Association Books, 1991), p. 151–2.

6. See 'On Animals', *Performance Research*, V, No. 2 (Summer 2000), passim. There is comparatively little work on wild animal circus acts, but see Paul Bouissac, 'Poetics in the Lion's Den: the Circus Act', *Modern Language Notes*, LXXXVI (1971), p. 845–57; and 'Behaviour in Context: In What Sense Is a Circus Animal Performing?' in Thomas A. Sebeok and Robert Rosenthal, ed., *The Clever Hans Phenomenon* (New York: New York Academy of Sciences, 1981), p. 18–25. My approach differs from Bouissac's semiotics in that it is more historical, paying greater attention to the statements made by the trainers themselves.

7. A. D. Bartlett, *Wild Animals in Captivity* (London: Chapman and Hall, 1898), p. 29–30.

8. [Ephraim Watts], *Citizen of New York: the Life of Van Amburgh the Brute Tamer with Anecdotes of His Extraordinary Pupils* (London: Robert Tyas, 1838), p. 36.

9. See Stephen Duffy, 'Landseer and the Lion-Tamer: the "Portrait of Mr Van Amburgh" at Yale', *The British Art Journal*, III, No. 3 (Autumn 2002), p. 25–35.

10. M. Willson Disher, *Greatest Show on Earth* (London: Bell, 1937), p. 146.

11. Edward Seago, *Sons of Sawdust: with Paddy O'Flynn's Circus in Western Ireland* (London: Putnam, 1934), p. 5.

12. Frank C. Bostock, *The Training of Wild Animals* (London: R. Brimley Johnson; New York: Century, 1903), p. 220.

13. Information from Dexter Fellows and Andrew A. Freeman, *This Way to the Big Show: the Life of Dexter Fellows* (New York: Viking Press), p. 239. See also Ellen Velvin, *Behind the Scenes with Wild Animals* (New York: Moffat, Yard, 1906).

14. Information from A. H. Kober, *Star Turns*, trans. from the German (London: Noel Douglas, 1928).

15. Sir Garard Tyrwhitt-Drake, *The English Circus and Fair Ground* (London: Methuen, 1946), p. 117.

16. John S. Clarke, *Circus Parade* (London: Batsford, 1936), p. 91–2.

17. Information from Willan G. Bosworth, *Wagon Wheels: the Romance of the Circus* (London: Heath Cranton, 1935), p. 93–100; see also John S. Clarke, *Circus Parade* (London: Batsford, 1936).

18. John S. Clarke, *Circus Parade* (London: Batsford, 1936), p. 95.

19. See David Lewis Hammarstrom, *Behind the Big Top* (South Brunswick; New York: Barnes; London: Thomas Yoseloff, 1980).

20. Fred Bradna, as told to Spence Hartzell, *The Big Top: My Forty Years with the Greatest Show on Earth* (London: Hamish Hamilton, 1953), p. 169.

21. A. Stanley Williamson, *On the Road with Bertram Mills* (London: Chatto and Windus, 1938).

22. For Togare see also Lady Eleanor Smith, *Life's a Circus* (London: Longmans, Green, 1939), Chapter 30; and Clarke, *Circus Parade*.

23. Information from Alex Kerr, *No Bars Between* (London: Cassell, 1957).

24. Information from Dexter Fellows, *This Way to the Big Show* (New York: Viking, 1936).

25. Clyde Beatty with Edward Anthony, *Facing the Big Cats: My World of Lions and Tigers* (London: Heinemann, 1965), p. 14–17.

26. David Lewis Hammarstrom, *Behind the Big Top* (New Jersey: A. S. Barnes, 1980), p. 25. See also Al G. Barnes, *Master Showman* (London: Cape, 1938), p. 243–8.

27. A. Stanley Williamson, *On the Road with Bertram Mills* (London: Chatto and Windus, 1938).

28. See Jimmy Chipperfield, *My Wild Life* (London: Macmillan, 1975), p. 10.

29. Alex Kerr, *No Bars Between* (London: Cassell, 1957), p. 166.

30. Gösta Kruse, *Trunk Call* (Elek, 1962), p. 100.

31. Fred Bradna, as told to Hartzell Spence, *The Big Top: My Forty Years with the Greatest Show on Earth* (London: Hamish Hamilton, 1953), p. 123.

32. See Antony Hippisley Coxe, *A Seat at the Circus* (London: Evans, 1951).

33. See Fred Bradna, as told to Hartzell Spence, *The Big Top: My Forty Years with the Greatest Show on Earth* (London: Hamish Hamilton, 1953), p. 164–5.

34. Norman Barrett, *Ringmaster: My Life in Showbusiness* (Harlow, Essex: Aardvark Publishing, 1994), p. 95.

35. For animals and their relation to distance see Dick Chipperfield, *My Friends the Animals* (London: Souvenir Press, 1963), p. 159–160.

36. Alfred Court, *Wild Circus Animals* (London: Burke, 1954), p. 61. However, some suggested that Court was asked to stress the severity of his training methods by his publishers. See Pamela MacGregor-Morris, *Sawdust and Spotlight* (London: H. F. and G. Witherby, 1960), p. 94.

37. George Conklin, *The Ways of the Circus: Being the Memories and Adventures of George Conklin, Tamer of Lions* (New York; London: Harper, 1921), p. 37.

38. Edward Seago, *Circus Company: Life on the Road with the Travelling Show* (London: Putnam, 1933), p. 118.

39. Willan G. Bosworth, *Wagon Wheels: the Romance of the Circus* (London: Heath Cranton, 1935), p. 105.

40. A. Stanley Williamson, *On the Road with Bertram Mills* (London: Chatto and Windus, 1938), p. 203.

41. Ibid., p. 100.

42. See David Lewis Hammarstrom, *Behind the Big Top* (South Brunswick; New York: A. S. Barnes; London: Thomas Yoseloff, 1980); and George Speaight, *A History of the Circus* (London: Tantivy Press, 1980), p. 183.

43. See Carl Hagenbeck, *Beasts and Men: Being Carl Hagenbeck's Experiences for Half a Century among Wild Animals* (London: Longmans, Green, 1909).

44. See J. Y. Henderson, *Circus Doctor* (London: Peter Davies, 1952), p. 90.

45. Dexter W. Fellows and Andrew A. Freeman, *This Way to the Big Show: the Life of Dexter Fellows* (New York: Viking, 1936), p. 235–6.

46. Frank Bostock, *The Training of Wild Animals* (London: R. Brimley Johnson; New York: Century, 1903), p. 215.

47. Frank Foster, *Pink Coat, Spangles, and Sawdust: Reminiscences of Circus Life with Sanger's, Bertram Mills and Other Circuses* (London: Stanley Paul, 1984), p. 139.

48. In his fictionalization of the trainer's life, *The Final Confession of Mabel Stark* (London: Atlantic Books, 2003), Robert Hough explains the trick by having Rajah sexually attracted to Stark: he ejaculates on her back.

49. J. Y. Henderson, *Circus Doctor* (London: Peter Davies, 1952), p. 51–2.

50. *Training of Wild Animals*, ed. Ellen Velvin (London: R. Brimley Johnson; New York: Century, 1903), p. 87.

51. Al G. Barnes, *Master Showman* (London: Cape, 1938), p. 247.

52. Clyde Beatty with Edward Anthony, *Facing the Big Cats: My World of Lions and Tigers* (London: Heinemann, 1965), p. 15.

53. Alfred Court, *Wild Circus Animals* (London: Burke, 1954), p. 56.

54. J. Y. Henderson, *Circus Doctor* (London: Peter Davies, 1952), p. 43.

55. Jim Frey, *Wild Animals and Their Secrets*, trans. from the French by Edward Fitzgerald (London: Muller, 1958), p. 36.

56. Ibid., p. 13–14.

57. Ibid., p. 217.

58. Clyde Beatty with Edward Anthony, *Facing the Big Cats: My World of Lions and Tigers* (London: Heinemann, 1965), p. 136.

59. Alex Kerr, *No Bars Between* (London: Cassell, 1957), p. xviii.

60. Ibid., p. xx.

61. Mary Chipperfield, *Lions on the Lawn* (London: Hodder and Stoughton, 1971), p. 94. In a sensational and well-publicized trial in 1999 the author of these sentiments was fined for causing unnecessary suffering to a chimpanzee.

62. Courtney Ryley Cooper, *Lion 'n' Tigers 'n' Everything* (Boston: Little, Brown, 1924), p. xviii.

63. Roman Proske, *My Turn Next* (London: Museum Press, 1957), p. 43.

64. Frank C. Bostock, *The Training of Wild Animals*, ed. Ellen Velvin (London: R. Brimley Johnson; New York: Century, 1903), p. 158–9.

65. Jimmy Chipperfield, *My Wild Life* (London: Macmillan, 1975), p. 58.

66. Ibid., p. 59.

67. Jim Frey, *Wild Animals and Their Secrets* (London: Frederick Muller, 1958), p. 164.

68. Frank Foster, *Pink Coat, Spangles, and Sawdust* (London: Stanley Paul, 1984), p. 128.

69. Alex Kerr, *No Bars Between* (Cassell, 1957), p. 96.

70. George Keller, *Here, Keller – Train This!* (London: Jarrolds, 1962), p. 137.

71. 'If man is a sapient animal, a tool-making animal, a self-making animal, a symbol-using animal, he is, no less, a performing animal, *Homo performans*, not in the sense perhaps, that a circus animal may be a performing animal, but in the sense that a man is a self-performing animal – his performances are, in a way, reflexive, in performing he reveals himself to himself.' See Victor Turner, *The Anthropology of Performance* (New York: PAJ Publications, 1988), p. 81.

72. John Lukens, *The Sanger Story* (London: Hodder and Stoughton, 1956), p. 49.

73. Frank C. Bostock, *The Training of Wild Animals*, ed. Ellen Velvin (New York: Century, 1903), p. 185.

74. Roman Proske, *My Turn Next* (London: Museum Press, 1957), p. 191.

Paul Dwyer

Augusto Boal and the Woman in Lima: a Poetic Encounter

Twenty-five years after the landmark publication of *Theatre of the Oppressed*, there is no denying the continuing influence of Augusto Boal on theatre practitioners, community workers, and political activists worldwide. To judge by the number of recent publications by or about Boal (including five best-selling books from Routledge in little more than a decade),[1] the 'Boal Boom' shows no evidence of decline. There is also, however, an emerging culture of critique around various aspects of the theory and practice of Theatre of the Oppressed; and in the following article, Paul Dwyer argues that a reflexive, critical approach to using Boal's techniques should begin with an acknowledgement that they are not based on a stable theoretical foundation. Rather, the underlying principles, articulated by Boal in the many anecdotes that fill his books, lectures, and workshops, appear to have shifted over the years to become more closely aligned with the expectations of his audience. The theory of Theatre of the Oppressed should thus be seen as a co-creation for which the readers and propagators of Boal's work share a significant responsibility. Paul Dwyer is a lecturer in the Department of Performance Studies at the University of Sydney.

The trajectory of Augusto Boal's work can be mapped as a series of epiphanies, a series of discoveries, a continuous process of response to his own perception of the inadequacy of what he was doing before; this is a very self-critical work, which thrives on problems. Viewed over its forty-year history, the work glides naturally, organically, from the socio-political to the socio-individual to the individual-political and back again – but it is always rooted in practice, and it is always theatre. The main body of theory, as articulated in *The Theatre of the Oppressed*, has stood the test of time, and is constantly refreshed and invigorated by the energetic, urgent extension and development of practice.

Adrian Jackson[2]

AUGUSTO BOAL'S reputation as a theorist rests largely on his earliest (English-language) publication, *Theatre of the Oppressed*. Whether or not this work should be taken on its own to constitute 'the main body of theory' underpinning Theatre of the Oppressed (or 'TO') practice is another matter. For one thing, the most explicitly theoretical section of the book, namely Boal's celebrated critique of Aristotle's *Poetics*, is more of a demolition job than a site of neat and tidy theoretical construction. (The fact that Boal, like Brecht before

him, offers some highly tendentious interpretations of Aristotle in order to articulate a counter-position to his 'poetics of oppression' need not concern us here – although it is odd that so many scholars have been prepared to take Boal's reading of Aristotle at face value.)[3] More to the point, it is unlikely that Boal himself, at the time of writing, regarded *Theatre of the Oppressed* as a 'naturally, organically' conceived corpus of key theoretical texts.

What we have in *Theatre of the Oppressed* is an anthology of production notes, field reports, and essays relating to an embryonic stage in the development of TO practice. In Boal's words: 'It is a theatre that has just been born, and which, though breaking with all the traditional forms, still suffers from an insufficiently formulated theoretical basis. Only out of constant practice will the new theory arise.'[4] Yet, as Drew Milne explains, this line of argument can be problematic: 'With practice the justification of theory, the theory's truth claims lie in qualities of practice which cannot be assessed as theory.'[5] Hence, Milne continues, it might be more appropriate (and in fact more in keeping with the subtitle of the earlier Spanish and

Portuguese editions), to consider *Theatre of the Oppressed* as a statement of 'political poetics':

Here 'poetics' is helpful, suggesting a middle term between theory and practice, caught between description and prescription. 'Poetics' suggests both theory and its intelligibility as description: theory as an abstract, formalized account of the *techne* implicit in *poesis*, and description of that which is intuitively and theoretically immanent in practice.[6]

It is my contention that Boal most skilfully negotiates this 'poetic' territory between theory and practice through his descriptions of various paradigmatic TO experiences – the moments of 'epiphany' to which Adrian Jackson refers in the epigraph above. However, these epiphanies are not 'gospel truth', or, at least, their truth cannot be separated from the moment in which they are narrativized and transposed by Boal into the form of a quasi-theoretical anecdote.[7]

Furthermore, since Boal has been rewriting and retelling some of these anecdotes over many years, it is possible to read into them something of the way in which audience reception helps to shape the development of a rationale for TO practice. In other words, to a certain extent we all hear the version of Boal we want to hear. I make this point since, no matter how 'self-critical' Boal may or may not be about his own work, it is unrealistic to expect from him all the answers to the challenge of practising TO in contexts far removed from those in which a so-called 'main body of theory' first evolved. Indeed, the situation now with respect to Boal might best be described in the terms which Heiner Müller once applied to Brecht: 'To use [him] without criticizing him is a betrayal.'[8] It is in such a spirit that I intend the following arguments.

A reflexive, critical approach – by practitioners other than Boal – to the development of TO theory and practice might best start by acknowledging the ways in which Boal's work is marketed internationally through conferences and academic publications, at theatre festivals, and on the workshop circuit. Certainly, his appearances in these contexts are framed by a significant level of consumer demand.[9] I can still recall quite clearly, for instance, the revealing turn of phrase with which Boal was

introduced for a session of the 1995 International Drama/Theatre and Education Conference (IDEA), in Brisbane: 'For the next hour and a half, we've got him – he's all ours!'

Later, during Boal's keynote address to this same conference, I found myself sitting next to a Brazilian academic who explained, firstly, that she had never had a chance to hear Boal speak in Brazil and, secondly, that his book, *The Rainbow of Desire*, had not yet been published in Portuguese (when it had recently appeared in English, and despite the fact that the first edition, published in French, was actually based on a manuscript in Portuguese).[10] Adopting the terminology of Pierre Bourdieu, we might think of the conference scene as an academic trade-fair, a privileged marketplace for the acquisition of *symbolic capital*. As with other markets, access to this trade in *cultural commodities* is not exactly free, and consumer demand does have some bearing on product development.[11]

A Political-Theatrical Problem

Now, as it turns out, Boal's keynote speech in Brisbane was essentially another retelling of the 'three theatrical encounters' which appear in the prologue of *The Rainbow of Desire* and which, over a period of many years, have come to stand as defining moments in the development of TO. For my present purposes, I want to focus very closely on a story which has been in Boal's repertoire for at least thirty years and in which the development of Forum Theatre is ascribed to his momentous encounter with a 'large woman' in the audience of a performance near Lima in 1973 (her exact physical appearance and behaviour, as we shall see, alter somewhat over the years).[12]

The analysis below compares four distinct versions of the story. Their sources are:

(1) From *Theatre of the Oppressed* – this version was written in December 1973 and first published in 1974. The quotations below are taken from the 1979 English text, a very close translation from the earliest Spanish text. Hence, I will refer to this as the '1973/1979 version'.[13]

(2) From *Méthode Boal de théâtre et thérapie: l'arc-en-ciel du désir*, published in 1990 – this version is referred to below as the 'French Rainbow Text' although, for convenience, it is quoted in translation.[14]

(3) From the English edition of *The Rainbow of Desire*, published in 1995 and referred to below as the 'English Rainbow Text'.[15]

(4) From Boal's keynote address, also in 1995, to the Brisbane IDEA Conference – referred to below as the 'Brisbane Keynote'.[16]

The story revolves around a workshop during which Boal and his fellow theatre workers are developing short plays in response to themes suggested by local community members. As he explains in the 1973/1979 version in *Theatre of the Oppressed*:

In a barrio *of San Hilariòn, in Lima, a woman proposed a controversial theme. Her husband, some years before, had told her to keep some 'documents' which, according to him, were extremely important. The woman – who happened to be illiterate – put them away without suspicion. One day they had a fight for one reason or another and, remembering the documents, the woman decided to find out what they were all about, since she was afraid they had something to do with the ownership of their small house. Frustrated in her inability to read, she asked a neighbour to read the documents to her. The lady next door kindly made haste to read the documents which, to the surprise and amusement of the whole* barrio, *were not documents at all, but rather love letters written by the mistress of the poor woman's husband. Now this betrayed and illiterate woman wanted revenge. The actors improvised the scenes until the moment where the husband returns at night, after the wife has uncovered the mystery of the letters. The woman wants revenge: how is she to get it?*[17]

At this point in the story, Boal describes opening up proceedings to the audience, who make suggestions to the actress playing the wife. She improvises them all, one after another, but none appears satisfactory – none, that is, until a 'large exuberant lady' gets involved.

Before looking at this woman's historic intervention, it is interesting to compare the above with the way the betrayed woman presents in the 1990 French Rainbow Text:

One fine day, a shy woman came to see me. She said: 'I know that you do political theatre, and my problem is not political, but it is a very big problem and it's mine. Perhaps you could help me with your theatre?'[18]

Five years later, for the English Rainbow Text, Boal expands on this conversation with the woman, adding the following paragraph:

I told her that, in my opinion, all problems are political, but she replied that this was not so in her case. Why? Because, she said, her problem was her husband. 'You see – you said "my husband", and who tells you that that man is your husband? Society married you to him, so your problem is political.'[19]

Finally, this conversation becomes even more animated in the following transcript from the Brisbane keynote:

A woman came to me and said 'Oh it's so nice that way [the way Boal and the actors would respond to suggestions from the audience], it's so democratic because all of us, we can say what we think.' And I said, 'Yes, did you like it?' And she said, 'Yes. The only thing that I did not like is because you only talk about political problems and I have a very big problem and this problem is not political. So you cannot do anything about it.' And I said, 'Madam, first of all, all problems are political. So you tell me what's your problem and I'll show you that we can do a play about it because it is political.' She said, 'No, no, my problem is not political.' And I said, 'I swear it is. Tell me what's your problem and I'm going to show you that it is political.' And she said, 'My problem is not political because it is between me and my husband.' And I said, 'OK . . . your husband – that's political, because who tells you that he's your husband? It's society. It's not "you and a man you know", it's not "you and somebody else". It's "you and your husband". And who can tell you that he's your husband? It's society. If society tells you that you are "his wife" and he's "your husband", your problem is a political problem.' And she was very happy and said, 'Oh, me and my husband, we are political!' I said 'Yes! Yes! As political as you can be! You are political.' And she said, 'So you can do a play about my situation?' I said, 'Yes we can do a play about you.'[20]

Over the years, then, Boal has been at pains to emphasize the political dimension of the woman's problem; but was she herself ever all that mystified? Back in 1973, there was no suggestion that the woman was ever labouring under any kind of ideological false consciousness. Her first, hardly naive thought is that the husband's documents might have 'something to do with the ownership of their small house'. She then experiences the humiliation of having all her neighbours learn about the husband's mistress. Yet, far from being cowed by this, she decides to socialize the problem she is experiencing and proposes it (apparently without hesitation) as a 'controversial theme' for the workshop. The woman knows what she wants – namely, suitable revenge – and hesitates only as to the means.

Enacting the Birth of Forum Theatre

Now, to pick up the story again where I left off, a 'large exuberant woman' enters into Boal's narrative. In 1990 (the French Rainbow Text), he puts it like this: 'Suddenly I spotted a rather large woman, seated in the third row, who was shaking her head and bursting with rage.'[21] For the English Rainbow Text, the woman becomes 'very large, powerful . . . built like one of those Japanese sumo fighters'.[22] Here too, she's 'shaking her head and bursting with rage'. In the Brisbane keynote, she is 'a very strong woman, but not that she was fat, she was – she had big muscles'.[23] By this time, she is also 'like a dragon throwing smoke!'

In all three of these versions, Boal admits to being afraid of the woman – in the French and English Rainbow Texts, this is on account of the woman 'glaring at me with a look of absolute hatred';[24] in the Brisbane keynote, more candidly perhaps, Boal is afraid of the woman 'because she was really strong'.[25] Nevertheless, Boal summons up the courage to ask the woman for her suggestion and in each of these versions he is baffled by her

response. The English Rainbow Text, for instance, reads:

'This is what [the betrayed woman] should do: let the husband in, have a clear conversation with him, and then, and only then, forgive him.' I was completely baffled. With all her huffing and puffing, and muttered comments, and looks that could kill, I was expecting her to propose solutions of a more violent nature. Anyway, I didn't argue, and I told the actors to improvise this new solution. They improvised, but without any real gusto. The husband protested his love and – all's well that ends well – asked his wife to bring him his supper. She went off to the kitchen and that's how the scene ended. I looked at the big woman; she was huffing and puffing more than ever and her fulminating glare was even more furious and murderous than before.[26]

In the Brisbane keynote, Boal describes the woman, by this stage, as 'really almost levitating'.[27] The actors try again to improvise a 'clear conversation' without making much progress and an argument follows (in the later English-language versions, at least – not in French or Spanish) in which the woman accuses Boal of sabotaging her idea 'because you are a man and men don't understand women and you are not understanding what I said because you don't want to'.[28]

Finally, the woman leaves her seat. In the French and English Rainbow texts this is to take up Boal's hesitant offer to come up on stage and act out the idea herself – he makes the same offer in the Brisbane keynote version although, interestingly enough, there the offer is made only *after* the woman has stood up to leave and out of Boal's mixed feelings of (a) relief at realizing she wasn't about to attack him physically; but also (b) pity at the sight of her leaving the theatre: 'Madam, please don't do that, don't go away. We are trying our best.'[29] In each of these three versions, upon Boal's suggestion that she come up on stage, the woman is 'illuminated and transfigured . . . "May I?" "You may!"'[30]

The story ends happily with the woman's bravura acting out of what she means by a 'clear conversation'. Here is the English Rainbow Text, plus one of Boal's own bravura ad-libs from the Brisbane keynote:

She came up on stage, grabbed the poor defence-less actor-husband (who was a real actor, but not a real husband, and moreover was skinny and weak), and laid into him with a broom-handle with all her strength, simultaneously delivering a lecture to him on her complete views on the relations between husband and wife. We attempted to rescue our endangered comrade, but the big woman was much stronger than us. [From the Brisbane keynote: She was so strong she did this to me. *(Boal mimes receiving an elbow to the gut.)* I went back to the setting over there, I ran over the setting . . . and then she kept hitting him and he was so Stanislavskian when he said, 'Forgive me! I'll never do that again!' And we believed him so well, he was so true to that.] *Finally, she stopped of her own accord and, satisfied, planted her victim on a seat at the table and said: 'Now that we have had this very clear and very sincere conversation, you can go to the kitchen and fetch my dinner, because after all this I'm tired out!'*[31]

Boal concludes by explaining how this intervention made it clear to him that 'when the spectator herself comes on stage and carries out the action she has in mind, she does it in a manner which is personal, unique, and non-transferable . . . as no artist can do it in her place . . . This is how Forum Theatre was born.'[32]

The Woman in Lima Transported

It is a good story – one that myself and other TO practitioners have told as part of warming up a Forum Theatre audience. However, the difference between the description above and the 1973/1979 version of the woman's intervention is also highly instructive. Here it is now, in full:

The last solution was presented by a large exuberant woman; it was the solution accepted unanimously by the entire audience, men and women. She said: 'Do it like this: let him come in, get a really big stick, and hit him with all your might – give him a good beating. After you've beat him enough for him to feel repentant, put the stick

away, serve him his dinner with affection, and forgive him.' The actress performed this version, after overcoming the natural resistance of the actor who was playing the husband, and after a barrage of blows – to the amusement of the audience – the two of them sat at the table, ate, and discussed the latest measures taken by the government, which happened to be the nationalization of American companies.[33]

So, in this early version, the woman does not appear to shake her head, to burst with rage, to throw murderous looks in Boal's direction, to breath fire, to levitate – or, indeed, to leave her seat. She does not need to get up on stage and show the actors what to do, since everyone has understood, quite clearly, what she has said. In the English Rainbow version of the story, Boal is 'baffled' (in the French Rainbow text and the Brisbane keynote he is even 'disappointed') when the woman does not propose a violent solution. Yet, in the earliest written version, she does advocate violence – it is only the actors who hesitate. Also, in this early version, the whole audience (men and women) are united in their delight – a far cry from the stand-off between Boal and the woman, as it is described in later versions.

In 1973, the explicit 'political problem' is not the socially defined relations between men and women; on the contrary, the actor-husband and the actor-wife discuss together the issue of the day: the nationalization of American companies. This might sound a little fanciful, a case of the actors improvising and steering the scene towards a politically correct happy end. (This raises the question, of course, as to whether the story's ending in later versions is any less politically correct – at any rate, the 1973/1979 version, more so than later ones, clearly sets the story in the context of a theatre-based literacy project, sponsored by the revolutionary government of Peru in 1973.)[34] Finally, if we are to follow the 1973/1979 version, Forum Theatre was *not* born on this occasion: Boal tells the story in his first book purely to illustrate the technique of 'simultaneous dramaturgy' and Forum Theatre is not in fact mentioned till five pages later.[35]

Testing Theory through Call and Response

In oral storytelling traditions, the performer listens out for what the audience wants to hear. So no two audiences should get the same story – indeed, this is a sign of respect. Certainly, part of Boal's effectiveness as a teacher is bound up with the way he is able to expand on his material in performance, slipping in and out of narration and enactment, varying his pace and rhythm, making sure his audience gets both the laughs and the more didactic punchlines. The facts of the Woman in Lima story are, partly, 'manufactured' – fashioned and re-fashioned by at least thirty years of performing, writing, editing, re-writing, translating, and so on. The story is a 'true fiction', to borrow James Clifford's description of ethnographic writing – a description which Clifford supports by citing both meanings of the Latin root *fingere*: 'making, but also . . . making up'.[36]

In highlighting these discrepancies between the different versions of the Woman in Lima story, I do not mean to suggest, however, that Boal has simply made the whole thing up. Perhaps the 1973/1979 version is the closest to what actually happened. Perhaps the later versions are an amalgam of several similar episodes. Or perhaps, as the theoretical significance of the episode has become clearer to Boal, he has added details which did not seem relevant before. Thus, in the Brisbane keynote, he remarks how

In the first moment, I saw the anecdotic [value of this episode] . . . It was a beautiful event. But then I started thinking – what has this woman done besides being enraged and going there [on stage]? Why was she so much enraged? And then I reflected about this – what makes theatre?[37]

Rather than seeking to establish, once and for all, the 'truth' of the matter, the main issue now is surely to understand the way in which the Woman in Lima story functions as a widely circulated pedagogical text. What do the shifts from one version to another signify about the relationship of Boal to would-be TO practitioners; and what do they signify about the changing context of TO practice?

To the extent that the story undergoes *systematic* transformations over the years, this might be a case of Boal revising and adapting the 'hypo-theses' derived from his earliest, raw experiences. As Bourdieu would have it, the 'logic of practice' means that such experiences can take on an extraordinary weight. It is as if they support an immune system which keeps us from enquiring too deeply into the assumptions governing our daily practice – all those thoughts and actions that come to us as if by 'second nature', making up what Bourdieu calls the *habitus*. The 'original' accounts of early experiences are enshrined because the *habitus* tends to be self-sustaining: it survives precisely by limiting our exposure to new or potentially disturbing information, places, events, people, and so on.[38]

Of course, a corollary to this would be that if we *are* exposed to new information, places, events, and people, the 'original' accounts are going to need some reassessment – and so, as Boal travels through Paris, London, New York, and Brisbane, the Woman in Lima is also transported out of her seat, her role in TO theory (as well as her physique) becoming more enlarged.

Jürgen Habermas suggests another angle here when he argues that ideology can deform discourse the way a neurosis manifests itself as a physical symptom on the body.[39] On this account, we might read Boal's changing description of the Woman in Lima's body as a sign of ideological uncertainty. Whether consciously or not, it seems that he does in fact rework the narrative at points which correlate to 'ideological fault-lines' in the transposition of TO techniques, from 'Third World' to 'First World' settings. Thus, among the more commonly voiced criticisms of Boal's work are, firstly, that his work in Europe and North America has become progressively depoliticized, moving into ill-defined areas of therapeutic practice, pandering to a bourgeois taste for individual psychodrama, etc.;[40] and, secondly, that his techniques rely on outmoded and restrictive binary oppositions between 'oppressor' and 'oppressed', between 'antagonist' and 'protagonist'.

On the issue of 'depoliticization', to charge Boal with selling- out to bourgeois individualism does, as Adrian Jackson puts it, smack of a somewhat 'ossified, unreconstructed Marxist reading of [his] movement into the therapeutic arena. . . . Therapeutic is not necessarily a synonym for normalizing or societizing.'[41] Nevertheless, many theatre workers seem unclear as to the rationale behind Boal's more therapeutic techniques and uneasy about whether they signal a radical new departure or simply an extension of earlier, more overtly political TO practice.

As far as Boal's reliance on binary oppositions is concerned, this view has been put forcibly by feminist practitioners of TO. Berenice Fisher, for example, argues that all too often Forum Theatre on issues such as sexual harassment or domestic violence reinforces stereotyped views of women as victims who collaborate in their oppression. When the basic rule of Forum Theatre – that spect-actors should only replace the oppressed protagonist of a scenario – is strictly applied, this could easily be taken to imply that women should be adapting their behaviour in response to violence rather than suggesting that men also bear responsibility for their own and other men's actions. Oppressed female characters, according to Fisher, are also frequently portrayed as so trapped and isolated within family structures that any 'attempts to break the oppression' are 'limited to individual heroics' – audiences tend neither to look for 'outside' interventions nor to challenge the 'individualistic, sexist or heterosexist assumptions built into the play'.[42]

It is, indeed, tempting to see Boal's alterations to the story of the Woman in Lima as a reflex defence against such criticisms. As shown above, on the one hand he drives home the point about the political nature of the relations between the betrayed woman and her husband (in effect, he substitutes a universally relevant political problem for the problems specific to the 1973 literacy project in Lima); on the other hand, he draws out the confrontation between himself and the woman in the audience to the point where it becomes like a joust between a diffident 'snag' theatre director and a militant, fire-breathing proto-feminist. Of course, this struggle bet-

ween Boal and the woman ends in a victory for both of them: he empowers her by bringing her onto the stage and she rewards him by enacting the birth of Forum Theatre.

Experience, Discourse, and Power

To argue the merits of one practice in relation to another means weighing up the value of different experiences (thus, Boal's encounter with the Woman in Lima yields a possible solution to the shortcomings of some earlier, agitprop style work in North East Brazil – the subject of another favourite anecdote).[43] And when Boal conducts a TO training workshop it is indeed a very rich lode of experience which he is able to tap.

However, the fact that these workshops are, in turn, so strongly based on a model of experiential learning (participants learn the techniques by doing them under Boal's direction and by working on their own personal experiences) means there is little opportunity to raise questions about the relationship between the context in which the techniques were first developed and those in which they might subsequently be applied. Participants can become so caught up in the process of 'self-discovery' (this being also one of the strengths of experiential learning) that they assume a commonality between their experiences and those from which the techniques derive.

In this way, there is obviously a risk that some participants might fetishize the heavily mediated images contained in stories such as that of the Woman in Lima. Beguiled by what seems to be an enduring 'authenticity', participants might draw on these stories, parasitically, to justify 'conventional' TO practice in a radically different context – rather than adopting the sort of critical attitude whereby changed circumstances might suggest novel practices.

Of course, it is not simply a matter of writing up new experiences to weigh against Boal's account of his foundational theatrical encounters. What is also at issue is the way individuals come to 'experience their experiences' in the first place. This is a more fundamental problem, highlighted by the feminist historian Joan Scott:

When experience is taken as the origin of knowledge, the vision of the individual subject (the person who had the experience or the historian who recounts it) becomes the bedrock of evidence upon which explanation is built. Questions about the constructed nature of experience, about how subjects are constituted as different in the first place, about how one's vision is structured – about language (or discourse) and history – are left aside.[44]

Scott's argument suggests that there is ultimately no way for TO practitioners to have direct access to the truth of the Woman in Lima story. As I have argued above, the interaction between Boal and his audience over the years actually produces a *different* Woman in Lima, a woman who no doubt better fits the image of an ideal popular theatre audience – passionate, rowdy, resourceful, unpredictable, etc. Whether consciously worked out or not, this rhetorical manoeuvre also fits perfectly with the logic of Boal's broader argument, advanced in *Theatre of the Oppressed*, that popular theatre has been in a state of almost terminal decline since Aristotle perfected his 'coercive system of tragedy'.[45] The 'birth of Forum Theatre', via the Woman in Lima's experience, rescues popular theatre from this fate.

More disturbing, however, is the fact that later versions of this story have also taken something away from the Woman in Lima. She is, quite literally, rendered inarticulate. She loses the capacity to explain what she means by 'a clear conversation'. And in this respect, Boal's restructuring of the narrative might be said to force her onto the stage in order to recover the voice that was always hers in any case. Without the ability to speak clearly, this woman – like the participants in a TO training workshop – must learn by doing. Such, at least, is the time-honoured piece of TO wisdom that the Woman in Lima story seems now to authorize.

Of course, there *is* a visceral charge which comes with deciding as an audience member to intervene directly on stage in a piece of Forum Theatre, to enact your desire to change a scenario which connects with some part of your lived experience of a particular social problem. There is a kind of knowledge – or perhaps, better, a will to knowledge and

power – which is apprehended in such circumstances and which is qualitatively different from knowledge acquired sitting in your seat as silent witness. However, there is no reason to conclude from this that the onstage intervention is *always* more telling than the discussion surrounding it, as if actions always speak louder than mere words. After all, whoever plays the role of 'joker' (or facilitator) in Forum Theatre, like Boal, generally does a lot of talking as part of their act. Taken in this way, the Woman in Lima story can still perhaps serve as a useful cautionary tale about the subtlety with which experience, discourse, and power relations become imbricated in TO pedagogy.

Notes and References

1. Routledge has published the following books by Boal: *Games for Actors and Non-Actors* (1992; revised edition, 2002); *Rainbow of Desire* (1995); *Legislative Theatre* (1998); *Hamlet and the Baker's Son* (2001). In 1994 they brought out an anthology of critical writing, *Playing Boal*, and a new study of his work is forthcoming in their 'Performance Practitioners' series.

2. Adrian Jackson, 'Translator's Introduction', to Augusto Boal, *The Rainbow of Desire: the Boal Method of Theatre and Therapy* (London: Routledge, 1995), p. xviii.

3 The outstanding exception in this regard is Drew Milne, 'Theatre as Communicative Action: Augusto Boal's "Theatre of the Oppressed",' *Comparative Criticism*, No. 14 (1992). Milne's close reading of Boal has passed without comment in at least two important anthologies of critical writing on TO: Mady Schutzman and Jan Cohen-Cruz, ed., *Playing Boal: Theatre, Therapy, and Activism* (London: Routledge, 1994) and *Contemporary Theatre Review*, III, No. 1 (1995), a special issue on Boal.

4. Augusto Boal, *Theatre of the Oppressed* (London: Pluto Press, 1979), p. 79.

5. Drew Milne, 'Theatre as Communicative Action', p. 114.

6 Ibid., p. 115.

7 Philip Auslander adopts a similar approach when he takes Boal's 'scattered and fragmentary comments on the body as theoretical texts' or, better, as 'accesses to important issues concerning the body in performance implied and engaged in [Boal's] work'. See Philip Auslander, 'Boal, Blau, Brecht: the Body', in Mady Schutzman and Jan Cohen-Cruz, ed., *Playing Boal*, p. 124–33.

8. Heiner Müller, 'Brecht zu gebrauchen, ohne ihn zu kritisieren, ist Verrat', in *Theater 1980: Jahrbuch der Zeitschrift 'Theater Heute'* (Seelze: Freidrich Verlag Velber, 1980).

9. To give an indication of the level of this demand, in the twelve-month period from April 1994 to March 1995 Boal spent more than four months giving workshops and appearing at conferences in the following countries: France, England, the USA, Italy, Austria, Germany, Switzerland, and Sweden. This was a time when he was also heavily committed to work as a *Vereador*, representing the Workers' Party on the Rio de Janeiro

city council. (The information cited here was sourced from an occasional newsletter produced by the Centro de Teatro do Oprimido, which operated from Boal's council chambers.)

10. As another keynote speaker to the IDEA conference, Rustom Bharucha, observed: 'Those of us who are located in the so-called "Third World" find that the routes of cultural exchange are already mapped for us, even before we enter them (if, of course, we are invited to do so in the first place). Invariably, we meet through the patronage of First World economies, which have the necessary capital, infrastructure, and technology to 'map' the world in the first place. . . . So, the "Third World" meets, if at all, through the "First".' Rustom Bharucha, 'Negotiating the "River": Intercultural Interactions and Interventions', *The Drama Review*, XLI, No. 3 (1997), p. 33. I understand that a Portuguese edition of *The Rainbow of Desire* finally appeared in 1997 – Boal refers to it in an online interview with Adriana Lessa de Miranda for *Theatre Network Magazine*, http://interlog.com/~artbiz/neterview1.html (consulted 5 April 2000).

11. Pierre Bourdieu, *Questions de Sociologie* (Paris: Editions de Minuit, 1984), p. 34–5; 133–6.

12. This story has indeed become so much a part of Boalian folklore that his theatre group in Rio performed a re-enactment of it as part of their contribution to the Seventh International Festival of Theatre of the Oppressed. See articles by Paul Heritage, 'The Courage to be Happy: Augusto Boal, Legislative Theatre, and the Seventh International Festival of the Theatre of the Oppressed', and Douglas Paterson, 'A Role to Play for the Theatre of the Oppressed', both in *The Drama Review*, XXXVIII, No. 3 (1994).

13. See *Theatre of the Oppressed*, p. 132–4. In an introductory note in the first Brazilian edition, *Teatro do Oprimido y outras Poéticas Políticas* (Rio de Janeiro: Editora Civilização Brasileira, 1975), Boal explains that this section of the book was composed first in Spanish in 1973. It was then published in Spanish in 1974.

14. Augusto Boal, *Méthode Boal de Théâtre et de Thérapie: l'Arc-en-ciel du Désir* (Paris: Editions Ramsay, 1990), p. 10–15. Where possible I use Adrian Jackson's English translation (see next note) – however, as my analysis demonstrates, there are occasional discrepancies between the two texts (including both cuts and interpolations, ranging from simple phrases to whole paragraphs). Where there is no direct correlation between the French and English editions, therefore, I have added my own translation.

15. Augusto Boal, *The Rainbow of Desire: the Boal Method of Theatre and Therapy* (London: Routledge, 1995), p. 3–7.

16. Augusto Boal, 'Theatre of the Oppressed: Politics, Education and Change', Keynote Address to the Second International Drama/Theatre in Education (IDEA) Conference, Brisbane, 1–6 July 1995. (Audiotape obtained from the Australian National Association for Drama in Education – my transcriptions.)

17. *Theatre of the Oppressed*, p. 132–3.

18. *Méthode Boal de Théâtre et de Thérapie*, p. 11.

19. *The Rainbow of Desire*, p. 4.

20. Keynote, IDEA Conference, Brisbane.

21. *Méthode Boal de Théâtre et de Thérapie*, p. 12.

22. *The Rainbow of Desire*, p. 5.

23. Keynote, IDEA Conference, Brisbane.

24. *The Rainbow of Desire*, p. 5; see also *Méthode Boal de Théâtre et de Thérapie*, p. 12–13.

25. Keynote, IDEA Conference, Brisbane.

26. *The Rainbow of Desire*, p. 5.

27. Keynote, IDEA Conference, Brisbane.

28. Ibid. See also *The Rainbow of Desire*, p. 6.

29. Keynote, IDEA Conference, Brisbane.

30. *The Rainbow of Desire*, p. 6.

31. *The Rainbow of Desire*, p. 6–7; Keynote, IDEA Conference, Brisbane.

32. *The Rainbow of Desire*, p. 7.

33. *Theatre of the Oppressed*, p. 134.

34. This was part of the ALFIN programme (*Operación Alfabetización Integral*), based on Freirean methodology. This programme is well described by Alfonso Lizarzaburu, a member of the then government's Educational Reform Commission, in his article: 'ALFIN: an Experiment in Adult Literacy Training in a Society in Transition', *Prospects: Quarterly Review of Education*, VI, No. 1 (1976), p. 103–10.

35. Details of 'the birth of Forum Theatre' are ambiguous in Mady Schutzman and Jan Cohen-Cruz, ed., *Playing Boal*. In their introduction, the editors maintain that Boal was using Forum Theatre in Brazil well in advance of his work in Lima (this later period being marked, for Schutzman and Cohen-Cruz, by the development of Image Theatre). Yet, in the same volume, in an interview with Michael Taussig and Richard Schechner (p. 22–3), Boal once again ascribes Forum Theatre's origins to events in Lima. This view is most recently endorsed in Augusto Boal, *Hamlet and the Baker's Son: My Life in Theatre and Politics* (London: Routledge, 2001), p. 309.

36. James Clifford, 'Introduction: Partial Truths', in James Clifford and George Marcus, ed., *Writing Culture: the Poetics and Politics of Ethnography* (Berkeley: University of California Press, 1986) p. 6.

37. Keynote, IDEA Conference, Brisbane.

38. Pierre Bourdieu, *Le Sens Pratique* (Paris: Editions de Minuit, 1980) p. 90 and ff.

39. Jürgen Habermas, *Knowledge and Human Interests* (Cambridge: Polity Press, 1987), p. 217 and ff.

40. See, for example, an interview by Lionel Pilkington, 'Dan Baron Cohen: Resistance to Liberation with Derry Frontline Culture and Education', *The Drama Review*, XXXVIII, No. 4 (1994), p. 17–47. See also David George, 'Theatre of the Oppressed and *Teatro Arena*: In and Out of Context', *Latin American Theatre Review*, XXVIII, No. 2 (1995), p. 39–54.

41. Adrian Jackson, 'Translator's Introduction', *The Rainbow of Desire*, p. xxi.

42. Berenice Fisher, 'Feminist Acts: Women, Pedagogy and Theatre of the Oppressed', in Mady Schutzman and Jan Cohen-Cruz, ed., *Playing Boal*, p. 189.

43. For a version of this anecdote, see *The Rainbow of Desire*, p. 1–3.

44. Joan Scott, 'Experience', in Judith Butler and Joan Scott, ed., *Feminists Theorize the Political* (London: Routledge, 1992), p. 25.

45. *Theatre of the Oppressed*, p. x.

Lesley Wade Soule

Tumbling Tricks: Presentational Structure and 'The Taming of the Shrew'

Much interest has recently been shown in the contributions of the actor in the performance of Tudor comedy. Lesley Wade Soule's subject is the larger performative framework of such contributions. Focusing on the main action of *The Taming of the Shrew*, she finds revealing examples of the characteristic presentational structures found in Tudor comedy, including direct audience address, mimesis as a pretext for presentation, a ritual/project structure, the use of stage personae, and a concluding ceremony of celebration. Her essay describes the nature of these structural elements, and offers examples of their functions in the play's performance as bodied forth in the text. Lesley Wade Soule is Senior Lecturer in Drama at the University of Exeter, where she teaches directing and the staging of Shakespeare. She has written articles on performance in the medieval and Elizabethan theatres and is the author of *Actor as Anti-Character: Dionysus, the Devil, and the Boy Rosalind* (Greenwood Press, 2000).

NEAR THE BEGINNING of *The Taming of the Shrew*, learning that the Players are to present 'a pleasant comedy', Christopher Sly has the following exchange with the boy Bartholomew:

SLY: Is not a comonty a Christmas gambold or a tumbling trick?
BARTHOLOMEW: No, my good lord, it is more pleasing stuff . . . it is a kind of history.

(Induction 2.132–6)

Despite Bartholomew's denial, Sly has raised the question of whether the ensuing comedy is to be a popular show performed by a company of stage players primarily for the pit or an illusionistic personation by actors of characters in an invented 'history' aimed mainly at the gallery.

In the event, *The Taming of the Shrew* provides both. While traditional criticism of the play has generally adopted the gallery perspective, in the play's own time groundling responses were central to both its intentions and its stage performance. A significant share of the text, and of the performance it implies and describes, confutes conventional illusionistic expectations, offering instead an old-fashioned popular show, clearly descended from folk festivities and farces, the Tudor interludes of fifty years earlier, and such

antic displays as those of Dick Tarlton in the 1580s. Like so many comedies of the time, *The Taming of the Shrew* was a composite of 'tumbling tricks' and 'history'.

It is only in recent decades that criticism and scholarship have begun to deal with what Robert Weimann describes as 'the question of how and to what extent performance in Shakespeare's theatre actually *was* a formative element, a constituent force, and together with, or even without, the text a source of material and "imaginary puissance".'[1] To consider this question it is particularly helpful to look at performances in the last decade or so of the century, just before the conspicuously performative components of theatrical presentation became increasingly overshadowed by the pleasures of illusionistic personation.

In considering this period, we must keep in mind Michael Bristol's observation that 'for the first few decades of its existence, the public playhouse of Elizabethan England was not fully differentiated from more dispersed and anonymous forms of festive life, play and mimesis'[2] – in other words, a theatre in which the presentational and the representational were freely mingled and by no means always fully distinguishable.

Elizabethan comedy embodied the confluence of two theatrical traditions, one of

NTQ 20:2 (MAY 2004) © CAMBRIDGE UNIVERSITY PRESS DOI: 10.1017/S0266464X04000065

popular non- and quasi-dramatic performance from the Middle Ages and earlier, the
other stemming mainly from the more illusionistic mimesis of Hellenistic and Roman
comedy. Representing the legacies respectively of Aristophanes and Menander, these
traditions, which may be called the presentational and the mimetic, involved on the
one hand a predominance of loose, celebrative performance and on the other of ordered
textual mimesis. Though both of course commonly involved use of mimesis, one tended
to give greater emphasis to the performers'
presence, the other to the 'history' being
represented.

Playing and Personation

The lively interaction of these two theatrical
tendencies in the writing and staging of
Elizabethan comedy provides an almost definitive paradigm of all theatrical performance,
as well as a fertile ground for exploring the
interaction of written text and stage performance. At the same time, the prominence of
the actors' presence in the Elizabethan theatre
raises difficult questions, several of which are
summarized by Weimann:

Where, in the script of dramatic representations,
do traces of performance retain an authority of
their own? How much of the strength of such dramatic representations derives from . . . performed
actions that are in excess of, even eccentric to, the
strictly representational uses of dramatic language
and yet able to conjoin the intellectual and the
material springs of theatrical production? [3]

Weimann's concern is in the context of his
interest in 'dramatic representations': such
questions take a somewhat different form
when one takes into account the primarily
non-representational patterns and structures
to be found in Elizabethan performance. One
effect of a long tradition of emphasizing playing over personating was that the staging of
plays (particularly comedies) made use of
performative structures derived from other
sources than textual mimeses. Looking at
Elizabethan comedy in particular, we are led
to ask: what are these presentational structures
occurring in the players' stage behaviour?

Since the representational and the presentational are closely blended in dramatic performance, the distinction between them is of
course by no means always clear. Particularly
in the Elizabethan theatre, the interaction of
two such fluid components in an actor's
stage behaviour was bound to be variable
and contingent. In any given performance,
the players' actions were a constantly changing composite of mimetic and quasi-, non-
and anti-mimetic functions.

Such multiplicity was actively encouraged
in various ways: for example, character texts
were commonly adapted, often by the players
themselves, to the varied talents of individual performers, just as fictional plots might
be altered to meet momentary presentational
considerations. The insertion into the performance of narratively irrelevant elements such
as solo and co-operative routines or *lazzi*, or
even mimetic interludes, was also commonplace. It is little wonder that, especially in the
early period, a play's performance was often
little more than a 'mingle-mangle', in John
Lyly's vivid phrase.[4]

The presentational structure of Elizabethan comedy was not merely a loose accre-
tion of varied elements, however. Certain
basic forms can be discerned, distinct from
those of the mimetic action and deriving
from very different sources. Even though presentational structure, by virtue of its nature
and varied provenance, is traditionally likely
to be less orderly than dramatic form, five
basic elements were usually present. Persistent in early popular comedy, they may be
regarded as definitive:

(1) direct address to the audience;
(2) using mimesis as a pretext for presentational performance;
(3) a non-dramatic project or ritual structure
functioning alongside the mimetic plot;
(4) the presence of stage personae, distinct
from and combined with mimetic characters;
and
(5) the inclusion of a celebrative conclusion
alongside or following the resolution of the
dramatic plot.

While these presentational elements commonly served to enhance the mimesis, they

all had, and were clearly intended to have, a contra-mimetic effect as well. The primary agency of this effect, of course, was the perceived presence of the player not simply as a character, but as a distinct stage persona, a presence amply (though of course incompletely) evident in the texts. In the public theatre performances of the 1590s, particularly in the staging of comedy, this presence and these elements of presentational structure were prominent – nowhere more clearly than in a play such as *The Taming of the Shrew*.

Addressing the Audience

The most obvious presentational structure to be seen in the performance of any playtext is created by those parts in which the performers interact directly in their own persons with the audience. This includes, firstly, direct address to and interplay with the spectators (often involving some kind of self-introduction and an explicit conclusion in the form of final bows or flourishes), and secondly what may be called the display of the performer's own physical acts of representation (distinguished from what those acts are taken to signify) – i.e., the overt presentation of the use of voice, movement, and gesture, including actions like singing and dancing which employ the text as a vehicle or framework. By such means, performers individually and as an ensemble establish and develop a structure of direct interaction with the audience.

At base, every theatrical performance is addressed to the spectators and is therefore at the primary level a direct rhetorical action, whatever its content. In the staging of most pre-modern comedy, this audience address was openly acknowledged, and the whole performance had an explicitly presentational nature. As in earlier, non-dramatic performances like carnival or festive ritual, the audience came to the theatre expecting a dialogic relationship with the stage performers. Mimetic representation (not, we must remind ourselves, the same thing as illusionism) was fluid. It certainly did not preclude the actors, in the course of the representation of a text, from openly addressing the spectators: they

could (and did) speak freely to the audience as either actor or character or both.

The whole presentational context of the performance was founded on the architecture of the public theatre, which, combined with the effects of daylight performance, located audience and players in what was recognized to be a shared public space. As in its theatrical and non-theatrical predecessors, the Elizabethan public theatre was designed in the first instance for public colloquy. As a result, stage representation inevitably had presentational and metatheatrical dimensions.

The use of direct address occurs from the start in *The Taming of the Shrew*. One of the simplest and most obvious instances is the handling of players' first entrances. The Induction (whose basic purpose has been to state, 'There is a play to come!') is followed by a flourish of trumpets ('The play begins!'), whereupon the actor playing Lucentio enters with his man Tranio (1.1.2) and conspicuously states the mimetic location ('fair Padua'), as the starting actor had done from earliest times.[5]

More specifically presentational is his 'I am arrived. . . .' Often taken as referring merely to the character's arriving at the fictional locale, the words also convey a presentational reminder to the audience: 'I have come onto this stage to address you out there.' By such simple means, the spatial-temporal premise of a physical here-and-now was established from the start, to be reinforced repeatedly throughout the performance by references to the theatrical place and occasion and to the audience's physical presence.

In plays like *The Taming of the Shrew*, the texts themselves were also structured towards direct audience address. One familiar and traditional means of doing this was the prologue, from classical times a device for establishing direct interaction with the spectators. Its expository purpose in relation to dramatic content is familiar, but its presentational function was equally important. This is apparent in virtually all early comedy, from the Old Comedy of Aristophanes (e.g., the opening scenes of *Knights* and *Frogs*) to Plautus (all of whose plays began with direct address prologues) to the interludes of the

Tudor period – of which the boy players' opening address to the spectators, 'Give room there, Sirs!' at the start of Medwall's *Fulgens and Lucrece* (printed 1520)[6] is a classic example.

Whatever its particular form, a prologue served to instruct the audience how they were expected to interact with the stage players – e.g., how much and how direct their interplay was likely to be – as well as to suggest how illusionistically the actors would handle mimesis, what were the particular conventions and parameters of performer–audience interaction, and how the players would treat the text (e.g., kinds and degrees of extemporization, theatrical irony, gestural amplification, and the like). By such means, the prologue established the norms of the performative relationship between stage and audience.

In the same manner, the Induction of *The Taming of the Shrew*, as an extended prologue, provided the spectators with numerous cues about how they were expected to relate to the actors. Sly's naive belief in the reality of his new identity and the comic 'history' he is shown, for example, offered the audience an ironic anti-model of spectation, while more sophisticated guidelines were provided by the Lord, his men, and the Players. The presence in the Induction of characters of different degrees of mimetic probability made it clear that the audience would be expected to adopt more than one perspective towards representation. Against figures from folk tales and popular performance (Sly and the Hostess) were set the traditionally (even literarily) mimetic Lord and his serving people, a contrast emphasized by their different languages and social class.

A third type of stage identity was normative: the Players, who, as both representational and presentational figures (i.e., both 'Players' and stage performers), bridged the styles represented by the other persons and prefigured the flexible interweaving of the mimetic and presentational which was to follow. Of particular interest was the introduction in the Induction of a crucial dual-function performer: the boy player – the page Bartholomew – who is given the task of impersonating a woman, along with detailed instructions on how to go about it.[7]

Why is so much emphasis placed here on the particulars of female impersonation? One intention seems to be that the boy's performance of Sly's genteel Lady should provide a clear contrast to the soon-to-be-seen shrew. Another, perhaps more important purpose may have been to give an audience already familiar with boys playing female characters a further, more pointed metatheatrical reminder of the dual presence of character and actor, particularly highlighting how the actor could play with representation. The double perspective introduced by this early performance of femininity in the Induction seems intended to sharpen the audience's awareness of the duality of the Katherina figure.

Frequent assertion of the player's presence is of course an essential part of maintaining direct address to the spectators. Considering all we know about the interplay between the Elizabethan player and his audience, and especially taking into account the date of the *Shrew* (1594 or earlier), we can assume (even without the many specific indications in the text) that the spectators were either directly addressed or openly played to almost constantly throughout the performance.[8] It is noteworthy that such direct address was used most frequently and conspicuously by the performers of the main taming action, above all Petruchio, who repeatedly addressed his action to the audience, often explicitly calling their attention to what he was about to do and had just done,[9] perpetually reminding them of his personal presence as player.

Many other similar instances, where the spectators were directly communicated with by gesture or look, though without explicit verbal address, are clearly suggested in the text.[10] The frequency of such address makes it clear that, for the spectators, being directly spoken and played to was a central part of their experience of the performance.

Mimesis as Pretext for Presentation

Comic performers have always played with mimesis freely and openly. In consequence, one of the staples of comedy has always been irony, in particular the theatrical kind. Comic texts tend to focus on amusing disparities between characters' perceptions of their own situations and of other characters, while performances of these texts often play upon contrasts between performer and character, and between the dramatic and the theatrical action. As a result, the performance of a comedy will usually have a clearly perceptible presentational dimension, a performative action providing an ironic accompaniment to the play's fictive plot. The primary agency of this irony of course is the actors' personal presence on the stage.

In the last decades of the sixteenth century, the actors of comedy generally handled mimetic representation without any serious concern for consistency of motivation or mimetic credibility. The play texts make this amply clear. So too does the reaction to 'personation' as it became increasingly popular. Thomas Heywood's enthusiastic response ('It is as if the Personator were the man Personated')[11] suggests that such belief had not commonly been the case theretofore. Before personation generated an increased emphasis on mimetic illusion and greater attention to details of the represented character, spectators focused their attention on the specific physical skills of the players and the embellishments with which they presented their rather casual characterizations.

The players themselves, besides enjoying their own skill and the audience response it evoked, were motivated in this highly presentational kind of acting by the traditional actors' desire to assert their independence of and superiority to textual mimesis, thereby demonstrating their primacy in the theatrical occasion: Tarlton remains a definitive example of this. At the simplest level, the comic actor's presentational play with mimesis has always involved simultaneously pretending and by various means calling attention to his own acts of pretence (a pattern of behaviour exactly comparable to the non-theatrical play of humans and animals, which combines make-believe and signals saying, 'This is make-believe').

Even while representing a mimetic action, however believably, the Elizabethan comic performer often engaged simultaneously in various kinds of openly non-mimetic play, including pure physical display, song and dance, or acrobatic combat. All of these were more easily accommodated if the principal mimesis of the text was kept casual and unsystematic, allowing freedom for actorly display.

Mimesis as Presentational Convenience

The presentational aspect of the players' performance was also enhanced by the frequent use of a kind of action which was neither purely non-mimetic (such as a dance) nor primarily representational (such as a dramatic scene), but readily lent itself to the ends of both presentation and mimesis. In action of this sort (of which the jig provides an example), mimesis was used, but essentially as a convenience, so that the players were only incidentally perceived as mimetic characters. They were seen primarily as stage personae – identities who were neither dramatic characters nor the actors as themselves. In this identity (a mode always available to stage actors) Elizabethan comic players would often shift into seemingly impromptu scenarios or *lazzi* – loose, casually mimetic actions of a kind which encouraged free presentational play: Launce's first appearance in *Two Gentlemen of Verona* (2.3.1–36) or the Porter's scene in *Macbeth* (2.3.1–24) are good examples.

Such actions were sometimes extended into complete little comic 'subplots' – e.g., in the jig, or Touchstone's extended interplay with William and Audrey in *As You Like It* (3.3; 5.1) – where clowning predominated, irrespective of the main mimetic action, which then came to be seen as a framework for various episodes of specialized comedic display. The traditional mimetic criteria of credibility, coherence, and causality were generally ignored in favour of the presentational values of display, variety, and exploitation of situation: entertainment took precedence over credibility.

In many early comedies, free play with mimesis was further facilitated by the use of familiar material from folk tales and medieval farce. (And action of this kind frequently included parody, by its nature a critical presentation of representation.) Examples are found in Udall's *Roister Doister*, where elements of folk festivity and liturgical parody are loosely packed into the external forms of Roman comedy, and in *Gammer Gurton's Needle*, in which the plot is little more than a casual pretext for farcical play. The very familiarity of such materials meant that neither close attention nor serious belief was demanded of the audience. Representation could be loose – even perfunctory – and something very different from the later, more intensive personation. In such plays, mimesis served primarily as a pretext for presentational action, allowing the performers to shift easily in and out of direct audience address, often adding ironic commentary on the mimesis itself. Specific acts of representation themselves sometimes became vehicles for freer presentation, which was thus kept firmly in the foreground.

The central action of *The Taming of the Shrew* consists largely of quasi-mimetic material of this kind. While a more self-contained, neoclassical kind of mimesis is used in the Plautine subplot, representation in the taming plot is loose and casual. The action itself becomes essentially a presentational scenario, loosely assembled after the Aristophanic manner, free and playful, often perfunctory, supplying both a convenient pretext and many opportunities for non-mimetic play. This casual and playful handling of mimesis in the taming action is the key element which keeps the presentational in the foreground of the performance as a whole.

The *Shrew* text also reveals a number of specific ways in which mimesis is used as a pretext for presentational play. In the Induction, the Lord's impulsive decision to play a trick on Sly by giving him a new 'character' is an obvious example of casual mock-mimesis, intended to provide opportunities for a display of actorly skills – in particular Bartholomew's ironic mimicking as Sly's 'Lady'. After the Induction, there is further playful manipulation of mimesis, primarily in the taming action. The very notion and representation of a 'shrew' are

playful, for example, as is evident both in Katherina's exaggerated performance of the type and in her mad suitor's cavalier denial of its credibility. Petruchio's frequent and arbitrary alterations of his own 'character' and his whimsical manipulation of other mimetic 'realities' (e.g., the various topsy-turvies of food, dress, and the identities of other stage persons) are further instances of the performers turning mimesis into presentational play.

Petruchio, Kate, and 'Mock-Mimesis'

The ironic impersonations of the Petruchio and Katherina players are of course the prime examples of counter-mimetic, presentational play in *Shrew*. These performances are mimetic representations, of course, but by largely substituting the conventions of popular clowning for those of dramatic impersonation they effectively mock mimesis. This ironic play with representation is prepared early in the play with the Petruchio actor's casual presentation of himself as a virtual burlesque of the typical suitor from traditional romance. After dispensing with the usual plot necessities, however, he casts aside conventional representation ('to the proof', 2.1.136) and steps into his true role as a stage persona: the madcap clown launching happily into playful combat with the equally theatrical shrew figure.

The adoption of such carnivalesque 'masks' by the two main figures is markedly different from the conscientious, rather literary disguises of the young scholar-tutor Lucentio and the pretended music teacher, Hortensio. The difference derives mainly from the fact that Petruchio and Katherina play assertive, clearly performative personae, obviously addressing themselves as much to the audience as to the other characters. Such figures always possess a stronger, more specifically presentational physicality on the stage. Because they openly play to both on- and off-stage audiences, they are seen as physically present *public* figures rather than, as with the lesser persons of the subplot, imaginary, absent *private* characters. The immediate and presentational, because it takes place *here* in the theatre, has always been seen as more public than the mediated mimetic, which purports to be happening *there*, in a separated elsewhere.

Dramatic Plot and Ritual Project

The pretextual, quasi-mimetic structures commonly found in comedy often took the form of projects, comparable to the performative projects undertaken by performers at fairs or carnivals, also chosen to suit the display of the celebrant-performers' skills. They often had a loose episodicity (as in Aristophanic comedy), which rendered irrelevant any expectation of causal narrative probability; and the greater flexibility of these essentially presentational constructs made them ideal vehicles for displays of a player's particular skill, be it ironic wit (e.g., by the Aristophanic anti-hero, Pierre Patelin, and Mak in *The Second Shepherds Play*), physical grotesquerie and dexterity (e.g., clown figures such as Hanswurst and the 'masks' of commedia), or, as in a piece such as *Gammer Gurton's Needle,* those of ensemble buffoonery. Most of all, such projects were seen as leading – like games or sports – to a clear physical outcome, involving a demonstrable triumph over clear, physical obstacles.

The very title of *The Taming of the Shrew* suggests to the audience that the taming action is to be presented not as a developed story, but as a simple project: a set of 'tumbling tricks'. The project-performer's objective is not dramatic – i.e., engaging in the ups and downs of a fictive courtship – but presentational: i.e., simply 'taming' her, a very specific, practical task with clear, simple means and parameters, and (as in most ritual projects) a predictable outcome. Entirely lacking the narrative suspense of the conventional mimetic plot, it is simply a vehicle for the display of theatrical skills.

This is amply clear whenever Petruchio and Katherina play together. Their 'scenes' have little or no dramatic interest or development: they are simply sketches providing opportunities for one or another variation on the basic comic routine of intersexual combat, rebellion, and subjugation. The taming

scenario has a form comparable to that of a circus performer's project, where the 'artiste' grandly announces to the audience his intention to bring his 'savage' victim under control; displays his bravado in a first confrontation; demonstrates his contemptuous freedom from conventional restraints as he engages in direct combat; then carries off his victim to his own personal circus ring, where he inflicts further comic humiliations on his stooge, before finally bringing her back to the centre ring for a last triumphant display by his fully tamed victim of the tamer's success.

In essentially the same manner, Petruchio's 'taming act' is boastfully proclaimed (1.2.90–2), embellished with progress reports along the way (2.1.310–13; 3.2.216–28; 4.2.159–82), and rounded off with a statement of triumph (5.2.186–7). How much the audience believes the taming to be a mimetic 'history' is incidental; what matters is their engagement in the immediacy of physical performance. Entirely lacking suspense or complications, the taming scenario displays instead a pattern no less familiar in music hall than in medieval farce: a succession of comic tricks by the clown and his stooge, leading to an entertaining finale and a bow to the audience.

The only possible suspense in such a project would lie in the question: will the performer bring off his feat of derring-do? The question is entirely hypothetical, however, for the conventions of non-mimetic performance (and the play's title) guarantee the outcome. The main action of *The Taming of the Shrew* therefore displays all the characteristics of a straightforward presentational project, virtually none of those of the traditional mimetic plot.

Storytelling on Stage

A common element in Elizabethan drama was storytelling, used both to further the mimetic action and as a means of characterization.[12] Particularly in comedy, stage narration often had an overtly presentational function as well. Launce's first appearance in *Two Gentlemen of Verona* (2.3.1–67) is a classic example of a domestic tale as performance routine. Such turns remind us of the long-standing prominence of the tale-teller as performer/character in folk tales and popular theatre.

In view of the taming plot's source in folk tale,[13] we are not surprised to find numerous examples of storytelling in the main action of *The Taming of the Shrew*, some brief, others more fully developed.[14] As we would expect, these narratives are given to the more clown-like personae, including Petruchio as the leading clown. At these moments, dramatic enactment is replaced by direct storytelling, accompanied by appropriate physical action by the performer: Gremio's account of the wedding (3.2.148–72) is an instance. Such routines are classic examples of Elizabethan stand-up comedy.

Mating Rituals and Folk Fantasies

The very familiarity of the quasi-mimetic scenarios used in pre-modern comedy – often involving a straightforward plan of deception or physical subjugation – was one of their strengths, for it freed the spectators from too much concern with questions of narrative causality or mimetic credibility, allowing them to focus on the immediacy of presentation. By virtue of their simplicity and similarity to each other, the projects had the quality of ritual, and like ritual they provided a form for the interaction of performers and spectators as co-celebrants.[15] In non-dramatic as in dramatic rituals, the emphasis has usually been on the specific (often prescribed) formalities of the leading player-celebrant's physical action.

For both symbolic and theatrical reasons, ritual performances frequently took the form of practical projects – e.g., the accomplishment of seasonal tasks or religious journeys – which also provided an element of narrative interest, often secondary. Examples can be seen in the fantastic journeys of Aristophanic heroes (to the sky or underworld) and in the symbolic combats of the Lenten carnival and other festivities.

Connections with fertility rituals are also found, and these are of course conspicuous in *The Taming of the Shrew*. Michael West aptly refers to the courtship/taming of Katherina as 'a kind of mating dance'.[16] With its male strutting, male-female play-fighting and eventual display of harmony, the resemblance to animal courtship is obvious.[17] The obviously ceremonial nature of this action renders modern considerations of sexual or social morality irrelevant. 'Criticism has generally misconstrued the issue of the play as women's rights', West remarks, 'whereas what the audience delightedly responds to are sexual rites.'[18]

In mating rituals, the participants are thus assumed to be complementary, different but fundamentally equal co-celebrants. Consequently, the frequent physical action in these rituals – of which Petruchio and Katherina's rough and tumble is a good example – are not representations of violence, but 'tumbling tricks'. What modern sensibilities are likely to perceive as bullying did not trouble unsqueamish Elizabethan audiences. The knock-about in *The Taming of the Shrew* is firmly in the tradition of early popular farce, in which physical conflict, often between male and female characters, was commonplace.[19]

Such sequences, only pretextually mimetic in comedy, were perceived by the spectators as effectively a kind of sport (compare the wrestling scene in *As You Like It* or the many swordplays in other plays) rather than as conflicts between a 'real' man and woman. They were seen as bouts playfully performed by male adult and boy players, co-performers well known and admired for their skills at just such stage rough and tumble.

Another ingredient of the quasi-mimetic presentational projects of early comedy was fantasy. Commonly found in folk tales and ritual, as well as in the earliest comedies of Aristophanes and his contemporaries, this often had both seasonal and allegorical significance. Also reflecting this background is the play with dreams (seen as early as in the dream of Pilate's wife in the mysteries), common in earlier Elizabethan comedies and seen again here in the Induction. The fantastic is also evident in the playful quirks of the whimsical Petruchio, with his casual disregard for practical and logical considerations of dress and behaviour. His fantastical appearance at the wedding, along with his 'magical' transformations of sun to moon and old man to young maid (4.5.1–22, 27–49), recall the proverbial 'wild man' of seasonal ritual, as well as the antics of Tarlton or of Diccon in *Gammer Gurton's Needle*.

Such feats of whimsical transformation are examples of how comedy (like the folk tale) from the earliest times played freely with mimetic or natural logic. Such playfully mimetic fantasies became liberated stage presentations, which incorporated both the inexplicable oddities of daily life and the free-wheeling vagaries of communal dreams, wishes, and fears. Like other elements of theatrical structure, fantasy took the form of casual mock-mimesis, yet another pretext for presentational display.

Character as Self-Fashioning

Just as dramatic characters are the agents of mimetic structure, serving as entities in the overall plot construction and as movers of individual actions, players and personae perform comparable functions in presentational structure. Dramatic characters and stage personae, as related but different kinds of theatrical constructs, interact in a particularly interesting way in pre-modern comedy. This is partly due to the unstable nature of dramatic character in the Elizabethan theatre. The modern notion of character as the fictive construct of a fixed individual and subjective identity did not yet exist.

Several early traditions thus continued to be active, especially in comedy: the classical notion of characters as exemplars of social and moral types was still prevalent, along with the Theophrastian character sketch and the medieval practice of explicitly allegorical characters. Even in life, at least in public life, character remained an essentially performative concept, aptly described by Stephen Greenblatt as 'self-fashioning',[20] by which is meant the development of a public identity through behaviour presented as performance. A definitive sixteenth-century example was Henry VIII, though his younger daughter was an equally expert 'self-fashioner'.

In the Elizabethan comic theatre, therefore, character was understood more from a performative than a mimetic perspective, that is, as what we would now call role: a set of stage actions performed by a player with a name-label attached, rather than the representation of an essentialist, subjective identity. In popular comedy, a theatrical character was perceived as a primarily performative construct. As S. L. Bethell has observed, 'The Shakespearean character may be thought of as telling his own story, with appropriate gestures and movement, from a standpoint well outside himself.'[21]

Such quasi-narrative characterization involved distinct mimetic and presentational identities, player and character perceived as closely interactive but clearly distinguishable. This mode of perception foregrounded the player, transforming dramatic character into a *theatrical* entity. Even the fictive component of the stage identity was clearly perceived as a presentation by what might be called the character's alter-ego – that is, the player's stage persona.

The essential provenance and locus of a persona is of course the stage: not as a platform of direct address nor as the specified imagined place of textual mimesis, but as a reflexive illusion. This becomes clear when we look at the most familiar example of a stage persona, the clown. Even when he was made a character in a play (e.g., Touchstone, Feste), the presentationality of this figure continued to be dominant. The same quality of being performing figures was found in other kinds of stage personae, such as the devils and vices of earlier theatre.

The attachment of a mimetic name and identity was perceived by spectators as a convenience, a vehicle giving the actor-persona new scope for his particular skills, whether of body, voice, or personality. This is evident with figures like Feste and Touchstone, Don Armado and Moth; it is also apparent with Petruchio, Grumio, and others in *The Taming of the Shrew*. Though often given fictional names in the plays in which they appeared, such figures sometimes retained their stage names. (Touchstone's name in *As You Like It* derived from Robert Armin's creation of a persona named 'Tutch' in popular entertainments and his original profession of goldsmith.)

The designations 'Clown' and 'Fool' are found among the *dramatis personae* of many plays, as are names from the Italian comedy, e.g., Grumio and Gremio. Even when given a mimetic identity, a name and an imaginary place of residence, a known stage persona remained a primarily public, presentational figure. In such cases, character became an obvious vehicle for presentational play.

Particularly in popular comedy, therefore, a character was responded to not primarily in terms of its dramatic credibility, but for its contribution to the stage show – that is, as a performer. Given the contingent nature of performance, mimetic consistency was relatively unimportant: a player could (and did) alter his fictive character to suit the demands and opportunities of performance. As a result, comic character was far more fluid as performed than as written, and more akin to the variable, improvisatory characters of Aristophanic comedy. Even the textual versions of Petruchio and Katherina strongly suggest such flexibility; we may assume that they were probably performed with considerable improvisatory freedom.

In the earlier comedies of the period – even those given a rough neoclassical form – fictional characterization is casual. In Udall's *Roister Doister* (1566/7) or Peele's *The Old Wives' Tale* (c. 1595), for example, plays typically cobbled together from a variety of sources, the characters show little credible consistency. In such cases, of which there were many, the vitality and unpredictability of the stage persona, even in reading, threaten to burst out of the neoclassical framework. In performance they probably did.

A Partnership in Comic Combat

Character as we now understand the concept must necessarily have stayed secondary until, as the century closed, mimesis was increasingly enhanced by a new manner of acting, i.e. 'personation'. In the comedy of the 'nineties, however, audiences did not require either 'believable' motivations or plausible consistency of behaviour. Their overriding interest was in the stage figure's immediate theatrical power, for which mimetic charac-ter was essentially a vehicle. In the immediacy of performance, therefore, the spectators' engagement with a stage persona (and even with many characters) was not primarily based on empathy with the imagined feelings of an absent imaginary person but on a pleasurable, physical identification with the presence, vitality and skill of the present stage performer.

It was this unmediated identity spectators primarily responded to, their response to the represented character being largely a spill-over from their basic identification with the player. It was the essential theatrical phenomenon of the actor's physical presence, well served by the canny theatricality of the text, which determined the essential nature of the main action of *The Taming of the Shrew*.

The leading figures in this action are preeminently presentational personages, given perfunctory mimetic characterizations with traits which were particularly suitable for flamboyant performative display. Making Baptista's eldest daughter shrewish provides an appropriate mimetic vehicle for the performance of aggressive courtship, as well as plentiful opportunities for comic ranting. Petruchio is given the character of a swash-buckling bachelor to place him in a productive performative relationship to Katherina: his braggadocio matches him to her shrewishness and gives him the opportunity to reveal his real theatrical persona of madcap bully-clown.

Their essential interaction is not courtship and marriage, then, but comic combat. For a contemporary audience, they were in the first instance a theatrical partnership of two well-suited stage personae: the adult vice/clown and the boy actor as irascible stooge. The pleasure given by both performers was of course enhanced by their doubleness as both impersonators and players. This duality not only increased the opportunities for exploiting their performative personae, it also allowed them to play these stage identities against the expectations associated with their mimetic roles: 'Of all mad matches never was the like' (4.1.231). Their doubleness enriched the theatrical irony of the contrast between representation and presentation.

Most of the figures of the subplot are more credible and consistent representations, more nearly characters than personae (although the mimetic consistency of some of them is imperfect, particularly the servants and the suitors when they undertake their disguisings). The main theatrical link between the neoclassical subplot and the popular, presentational sphere of Petruchio and Katherina is provided not by the familial connections of the mimesis, but mainly by the 'clownish servants' (the term used in *Two Gentlemen of Verona* applies here). As so often in pre-modern comedy, these are stage personae in barely fictionalized roles, their 'character' limited to their servant function.

In the comic tradition from Aristophanes onwards, servants – being of the 'lower sort' with which (according to Aristotle) comedy was supposed to be concerned – were invariably given greater freedom to violate mimetic consistency and illusion, and to play openly with the spectators. Perceived to be closer to the audience, they were facilitators of the presentational, and their actions were often comparatively independent of the main mimetic action. They often had the task of accompanying and providing a presentational framework for the fictive action.

This function is most familiar in the 'masks' of commedia dell'arte, who, while the *inamorati* carried on the necessary romantic-mimetic plot, had only minor mimetic duties, their main employment being to provide interludes of free-wheeling *lazzi*, sometimes mocking the mimesis, sometimes entirely unrelated to it. These figures were known to the Elizabethans: Heywood's *Apology* speaks of 'all the Doctors, Zawnyes [Zannis], Pantaloons, Harlekeenes, in which the French, but especially the Italians, have been excellent'.[22]

In *The Taming of the Shrew,* Grumio, Curtis, and Petruchio's other servants, together with (to a lesser extent) Biondello, are from this theatrical tradition and perform a similar function, though they are kept in a closer subservience to their master's actions than was often the case in the commedia. They remain primarily presentational figures, however, serving as Petruchio's entourage of supporting farceurs – stooges given occasional opportunities to step forward and perform their own comic *lazzi*, as, for example, does Grumio in the opening scene of Act Four (lines 1-90).

That these 'masks' are less prominent in *The Taming of the Shrew* than in the Italian comedy is due not only to the play's having two plots, but more importantly to the fact that the main plot itself is fundamentally a clown-like performance, consisting as it does largely of a thematically linked series of *lazzi* by two principal figures who are themselves 'masks' elevated to leading roles.

Petruchio

The conventional perception of Petruchio as romantic suitor in the mimetic plot has generally distracted attention from his function as a stage persona. In actuality, he has little in common with the traditional suitors of romantic comedy, being associated rather with the trickster figures of earlier popular performance. His forebears are Mak, Pierre Patelin, and the braggart soldiers of classical, Tudor and Italian comedy. Along with Katherina, he descends from the folk devil (e.g., 3.2.145–6) of so many popular tales and performances.

Perhaps his most obvious ancestor is the Tudor vice (himself among the progeny of the medieval devil). Petruchio performs all the business of the vice: the bombastic entrance, playful audience address, the loud mock-threats, and outlandish gear. His announcement on arrival – 'I have thrust myself into this maze, / Happily to wive and thrive as best I may' (1.2.52–3) – echoes the first line of Mischief in *Mankind*: 'I am cumme hedyr to make yow game.'[23] Arriving at his own wedding in outlandish gear, Petruchio reminds us of the vice Ambidexter in *Cambises*, entering with 'an old capcase on his head, an old pail about his hips for a harness, a scummer and a potlid by his side, and a rake on his shoulder'.[24]

Like the Vice, too, Petruchio plays blatantly to the audience and takes performative liberties with situation, character, language, and mimetic consistency. His comic aggressiveness echoes not only the vice, but also Herod and the devil. Most of all, he may well have reminded his audience of their recently departed favourite, another of the vice's descendants, the beloved, belligerent Dick Tarlton, described by one critic as 'a surrogate Lord of Misrule'.[25]

Petruchio shares another interesting trait with his vice and clown progenitors: he is a travelling figure. After providing perfunctory information about his father and his circumstances, he places himself as someone from an almost fanciful elsewhere, blown by 'such wind as scatters young men through the world' (1.2.47) to stir things up in this ordinary, everyday place – not simply Padua but this stage, which in such moments becomes an illusory self-reflection. The 'Bedlam' Diccon in *Gammer Gurton's Needle* makes a similar arrival ('Many a mile have I walked, divers and sundry ways'),[26] as does Ambidexter in Preston's *Cambises*: 'Thus do I run this way and that way.'[27] There is the quality of fairy tale and folk farce in Petruchio's free, sweeping movement from place to place. Having ebulliently won his shrew, he dashes off to Venice, makes an Arlecchino-like reappearance for the wedding, then whisks her off like Bluebeard to his own distant lair.

In his first appearances, Petruchio perfunctorily goes through the motions of the perfectly conventional – if rough – young suitor, but his presentational identity soon takes over. As he casts aside the details of marriage negotiation ('Ay, to the proof . . . ', 2.1.136), he ceases to be a character defined by fictional relationships and is seen for what he is, a comic stage persona, defined by performative criteria. This is not a character change, but a purely theatrical shift from mimetic character to presentational persona, with appropriate adjustments of behaviour, language, and particularly of his relationship to on- and offstage spectators.

Thus established early, his explicit presentational interplay with the audience continues to the end of the play. His dramatic character, being of minimal importance in the total make-up of his theatrical identity, is only perfunctorily sketched; his motivation is of the simplest, crudest kind, with no trace of psychological depth or complexity. From the outset, his wooing is presented as without personal feeling for Katherina ('She moves me not', 1.2.68), for he has only 'come to wive it wealthily in Padua' (1.2.72), though his briefly mentioned interest in wealth seems mere lip service. It is not greed but the challenge of the project that spurs him:

For I will board her though she chide as loud
As thunder when the clouds in autumn crack.
(1.2.91–2)

Like Mak's desire to trick his fellow shepherds or Pierre Patelin's wish to dupe the tailor, which have little to do with hunger or any real need for clothing, this is another example of how popular farce shows no interest in credible psychological motivation. As with all stage personae, Petruchio's prime motivation is to display his skill. His frequent boasts of what he will do (and has done) are not elements of dramatic characterization or plot construction, but simply parts of the performer's self-presentation to the audience. This being so, any tendency spectators might have to identify (and identify with) him as a dramatic character becomes irrelevant.

Neither he nor his mate belong in the mimetic world of Padua, as the reactions of other characters make clear: 'Nay, let them go – a couple of quiet ones!' exclaims Baptista (4.1.229). Standing as he does outside the requirements of mimetic verisimilitude and lacking the feelings an audience might expect in a fully dramatic character, Petruchio's relationships with the other characters (including Katherina) are not 'personal' but professional. To this overwhelmingly presentational performer, they are all stooges, victims, or admiring spectators.

Katherina

Like Petruchio, the figure of Katherina has a double identity, though with an extra dimension. First, there is the difference between two mimetic figures: the shrew and the young gentlewoman described in the Induction and who does emerge in Katherina's final self-presentation (and is imperfectly modelled by Bianca in the interim). This contrast, while it is between two mimetic identities, none the less has strong presentational implications, since the question of how a woman should be impersonated has been raised in the Induction.

The second dichotomy in the Katherina figure is between the female character and the boy player, including their differences of gender and age (though to Elizabethan spectators the age difference would have seemed slight). The Induction has prepared the audience for both dualities. The foregrounded example of a boy playing a female has reminded them of the actor-character gender difference, while offering them a model of a more properly performed (i.e., well-behaved) woman to contrast with the soon-to-appear and badly behaved (i.e., wrongly performed) shrew.

Once the main action has begun, it becomes immediately clear that, despite what has appeared in the Induction, the leading boy player will not subdue his behaviour to suit the conventions of female impersonation. His performance from the start has a pronounced presentational dimension, for the boy not only presents an outrageously shrewish character, but also displays his stage persona as 'misbehaving boy player'. The first appearance of the Katherina figure is therefore a show not simply of 'shrewish' bad temper, but also (particularly in the vocal and bodily elements of the performance) of a boy player's egregious misconduct. His first words are not only disobedient and ill-tempered, but also spoken considerably louder than those of the others, a delivery that would have been perceived not only as outrageously 'unfeminine' but also performatively dissonant with the other players:

I pray you, sir, is it your will
To make a stale of me amongst these mates?
(1.1.57–8)

Gentlewomen – and boys personating gentlewomen – were expected to speak 'with soft low tongue and lowly courtesy' (Ind. 1.110) or keep silent (as Bianca does in this first scene), but here not only the shrew but also the boy player's own performative voice is heard, angrily demanding that he be listened to as well as the character. This young performer has clearly declared his difference from the mimetically and theatrically well-behaved Page of the Induction. From Katherina's first entrance, therefore, the audience was shown not only a turbulent female but also a turbulent player.

As a woman with a reputation for outrageous conduct, a shrew was not only a type of disagreeable female but also a person whose bad behaviour provided entertainment for those around her: 'That wench is stark mad, or wonderful froward', says Tranio (1.1.69). The shrew was a public figure, with ancient and familiar theatrical ancestors, the most famous being Noah's wife. Moreover, just as Petruchio belonged to the vice's theatrical family, Katherina was a descendent of the devil. 'From all such devils, good Lord deliver us!' exclaims Hortensio (1.1.66), expressing the common notion that misbehaving women (and other misfits) may actually have been possessed. In view of the duality of character and player, it seems quite possible too that Katherina's devilishness may also have been associated by spectators with the well-known offstage devilry of boy players and apprentices.[28]

The Boy Player's Project

Katherina's character and its personation paralleled the duality of theatrical traditions found in the play. As Ann Thompson has noted, the 'wench' (like the shrew) is from the folk tradition, the 'maid' from classical comedy.[29] The distinction between these two types of female characters expresses and parallels that between the contrasting functions of the boy performer in the Elizabethan theatre: as boy actor, he was a credible personator of women; as boy player, he was a saucy mini-clown, presenting a lively stage persona in the popular tradition.

As also in the playing of such 'unfeminine' Shakespearean women as Tamora, Joan of Arc, and Margaret, the boy player here probably had to have great physical energy and vocal power, along with the ability to convey passion and a sometimes savage irony. These performative powers are consummated in the boy player's representational project by his ultimate accomplishment of skilfully impersonating Katherina as a proper gentlewoman.

The boy player's performance project involved two parallel tasks. The first, indicated by the title, was to present a rendition of an obstreperous female unwillingly subjected to male correction and control. His second task was to play the stage persona of recalcitrant boy player, presenting a lively burlesque of female impersonation, then 'compelled' to do it correctly. In this context, the Petruchio performer was therefore perceived as both tamer and teacher – not only courting and subduing a fictive shrew, but also taming and training a miscreant boy player. (The latter task is lightly prefigured in the Lord's instructions for Bartholomew: Ind. 1.101–26.)

A contemporary audience may well have seen the Petruchio-Katherina relationship as one between master and apprentice, a common situation in theatre companies at the time. Appropriately enough, the two players also shared a third project: to collaborate effectively in the presentation of a duet of comic combat, for their fundamental presentational objective was to achieve and demonstrate a successful theatrical partnership, as both characters and players. The boy may be thought to have had the harder task: he had not only to show his ability both to mock and eventually emulate the conventional mimesis of female characters, while simultaneously displaying the troublesome irascibility and professional skill of a boy player, he had to do all these while carrying on a sustained comic interplay with his fellow performer (and possible offstage master).

In their partnership, the boy's task was to serve as comic foil and stooge for the adult performer of Petruchio. While the man played the traditional ironic sharp fool,[30] the boy was called upon to perform a female equivalent of the braggart-buffoon's role. Its specific tasks were to provide enough loud self-assertion to counterbalance Petruchio's comic power of subjection, enough rough speech to provoke and counterpoint his bombastic rhetoric, and enough impotent rage to set off his displays of satisfied triumphalism.

Together the two figures presented yet another version of the traditional battle of the sexes found in the Adam–Eve scenes in the twelfth century *Adam* and subsequent medieval mysteries and farces. The woman (i.e., boy), the rebellious one, always shouted angry complaints and always raised new mischief. In the end, in both mimesis and performance, there was always a restoration of amicability and partnership, which was inevitably based on the man's subjugation of the female boy. Both the boy player and the quasi-mimetic character he was playing are presented as apprentices in the art of clowning, both learning to obey and emulate the mad master-clown:

PETRUCHIO: I say it is the moon.
KATHERINE: I know it is the moon . . .
> And the moon changes even as your mind.
> What you will have it nam'd, even that it is;
> And so, it shall be so for Katherine.
>> (4.5.15, 20–2)

In learning clownery, the boy could now play the female role as the world expected, but without losing his freedom as a player to take liberties, while his character learned how to love and be both obedient and free

Plot Resolution and Ritual Celebration

At the end of the play's penultimate scene, the mimetic plot is conventionally resolved: the young men win their lady loves and the old suitor is shamed and rejected. But in the following, epilogic scene, there is an ironic twist, for neither Bianca nor the Widow behave as mimetic (and worldly) convention requires. A neat crossing of lines has been constructed, Katherina proving a model wife and the 'gentle' Bianca turning disobedient shrew. In a manner appropriate to popular (as opposed to neoclassical) comedy, the improvisatory vitality of performance subverts the literary predictability of conventional mimesis.

Much modern critical discussion has focused on the apparent resolution of the Katherina character, in particular the question of how the long final speech about wifely obedience should be performed. Without retracing familiar arguments, I would like to suggest that this speech, along with the whole question of the character's resolution, can be better understood when seen as paralleling the boy player's presentational project. To assume that what the Katherina character is doing is both voluntary and sensible provides a key to both the interpretation and the playing of the scene. The character's acceptance of her master's dominance is premised on love, and her final speech is a conventional description of an ideal marriage of the time. Such obedience would have been seen as representing the rightful order of things. Coppelia Kahn asserts that the fictional Katherina is 'outwardly compliant but inwardly independent', and that the play shows that 'woman remains untamed, even in her subjection'.[31] The boy actor would have displayed this in his performance.

In the boy player's presentational project, an analogous resolution takes place. His playing of the final scene would have been partly perceived by the audience in the context of the task laid out for him in the Induction: to perform a proper impersonation of a gentlewoman. In his performance of his final speech, the young player was giving an ultimate demonstration of his impersonative skills. Starting with a display of outrageous shrewishness, he has moved through a considerable range of comic performance all the way to this composed completion, now showing the audience that he was more than capable of obeying the Lord's prescription in the Induction that the boy player should

> bear himself with honourable action
> Such as he hath observed in noble ladies
> Unto their lords . . .
> With soft low tongue and lowly courtesy.
> (Ind. 1.106–8, 110).

In defiance of early expectations, he has presented his authoritative impersonation of a gentlewoman. The theatrical irony is similar to that found in Rosalind's epilogue to *As You Like It*, where the boy player toys both with gender and audience.[32] In the final analysis, the ironic counterpointing of mimesis and performance in both plays is neat: woman and player alike are expert at simulating obedience, all the while taking subversive liberties with text and audience.

At the end of *The Taming of the Shrew*, we see further evidence of the close link between the presentational tradition and ritual celebration. From Aristophanes through the Renaissance, comedies nearly always ended with a celebrative ritual of some kind – a wedding, a feast, a dance, and sometimes all three. This ritual belongs both to the occasion of theatrical performance and to the comic project itself, for such an ending was a celebration by the hero and/or his associates of its successful completion. Such a traditional conclusion is found in the many epilogues of Elizabethan comedy and in variant form (until about the end of the sixteenth century) in the jig, a theatrical rite celebrating comic vitality and human fertility.

Before and after the time of the jig, these concluding ritual-performative celebrations were frequently incorporated into the mimetic action, often quite loosely, sometimes by having the celebrative epilogue spoken by a dramatic character suddenly become a presentational performer (which accounts for the mimetically rather improbable abruptness of many final scenes in comedy). In such cases, a presentational resolution occurs amounting to a reaffirmation of the celebrative compact made at the outset with the spectators. The final phase of *The Taming of the Shrew* shows the same traditional pattern of final celebration. The main taming action, the play's main presentational project, is effectively concluded with Katherina's kiss (5.1.123) and Petruchio's closing couplet:

Is not this well? Come, my sweet Kate,
Better once than never, for never too late.
(5.1.124–5)

At this point, the presentational project appears to be completed. But the Petruchio and Katherina players must still do a final turn for their offstage and onstage audiences, a conclusive demonstration of their success. While the celebrative final banquet and the wager (yet another game) are superfluous to the mimetic plot, they are important contributions to the satisfactory completion of the presentation. Included in this final display is a sting-in-the-tail epilogue to the subplot, as Bianca and the Widow revert to (it is whimsically suggested) woman's natural state of shrewishness, a view of the sex more consistent with folk tales and popular performance than with neoclassical comedy. At the same time, along with the Katherina player's display of impersonative mastery, this constitutes an ironic assertion of the influence and authority of the player, his freedom both to manipulate and mock the conventions of mimetic narrative.

In such testimonies to the players' freedom, *The Taming of the Shrew* plays to its last moments with the irony fundamental to all theatrical performance. To the very end, representation and presentation are intertwined, contrasted, and resolved, their difference and interdependence reaffirmed.

Notes and References

1. Robert Weimann, *Author's Pen and Actor's Voice: Playing and Writing in Shakespeare's Theatre* (Cambridge: Cambridge University Press, 2000), p. 5.

2. Michael Bristol, 'The Festive Agon', in *Twelfth Night* ('New Casebooks'), ed. R. S. White (New York: St Martins Press, 1996), p. 73.

3. Weimann, *Author's Pen and Actor's Voice*, p. 37.

4. John Lyly, Prologue to *Midas*, *The Complete Works of John Lyly*, ed. Warwick Bond (Oxford: Clarendon Press, 1902), III, p. 115

5. The statement of fictional locale (like the storyteller's opening establishment of place) is also an assertion of authority, for it carries the implication that, as creators of the mimesis, the performers can and will play with it as they wish.

6. Henry Medwall, *Fulgens and Lucrece*, in *English Moral Interludes*, ed. Glynne Wickham (London: Dent, 1976), p. 46.

7. Much more detail about personating a gentlewoman is given in *The Shrew* than in *A Shrew*.

8. Most – but by no means all – such direct addresses are by the more obviously performative figures: the servant clowns, Petruchio, and Sly. See, among many others, Ind. 2.63–9, 121–3; 1.1.78–9; also Grumio's many asides, such as 1.2.13–14, 32–3, 123–4; 4.1.1–8; etc.

9. See for example 1.2.190–204; 2.1.164–77, 291–302; 4.1.159–82; 4.3.165–72; 5.2.116–120.

10. Though Elizabethan players would certainly have taken even more opportunities than these to play to the audience, the following are a few of the most obvious examples: 1.1.105–6, 213; 1.2.5–19, 32–3, 211; 2.1. 242–51, 393–400; 3.1.45–47, 59–60, 84–9; 3.2.30–76, 195, 207; 4.1.1–8 ff, 91–158 passim; 4.3.1–14,190; 4.4.100–3; 4.5.35, 77–9; 5.1.33–4, 113–14; 5.2.136–79, 189.

11. Thomas Heywood, *An Apology for Actors*, with introduction and bibliographical notes by Richard H. Parkinson (Delmar, N.Y.: Scholars' Facsimiles and Reprints, 1978), B3 verso.

12. See S. L. Bethell, *Shakespeare and the Popular Tradition* (New York: Staples Press, 1944), p. 72.

13. See Jan Harold Brunvand, 'The Folktale Origin of *The Taming of the Shrew*', *Shakespeare Quarterly*, XVII (1966), p. 345–59 for a thorough discussion of these sources.

14. See for example Biondello's account of Petruchio's arrival for the wedding in his outlandish dress (3. 2. 41–62); Gremio's description of Petruchio's behaviour during the wedding ceremony (3.2.139–72) and Grumio's of the horse-fall incident, in comic competition with Curtis (4.1.38–65).

15. In early comedies, as in many seasonal rituals, the comic project often symbolized an important task: e.g., saving Athens in Aristophanes' *Frogs*, or killing Winter in medieval German carnival.

16. Michael West, 'The Folk Background of Petruchio's Wooing Dance: Male Supremacy in *The Taming of the Shrew*', *Shakespeare Studies* (Albuquerque, N.M.), VII (1974), p. 66.

17. From the choruses of Aristophanes to the *lazzi* of commedia dell'arte mask figures, emulations of animal behaviour have always figured prominently in comic performance.

18. West, 'The Folk Background of Petruchio's Wooing Dance', p. 71.

19. See for example Gammer Gurton's battle with Dame Chat in Mr. W[illiam] S[tevenson], *Gammer Gurton's Needle*, in *Elizabethan and Stuart Plays*, ed. C. R. Baskervill, V. B. Heltzel, and A. H. Nethercot (New York: Holt, 1934), p. 62–3; or Marian May-be-good's beating the vice Ambidexter in Thomas Preston, *A Lamentable Tragedie . . . of Cambises* , ibid., p. 162–3.

20. See Stephen Greenblatt, *Renaissance Self-Fashioning: from More to Shakespeare* (Chicago: University of Chicago Press, 1980).

21. Bethell, *Shakespeare and the Popular Tradition*, p. 72

22. Heywood, *An Apology for Actors*, E2 verso.

23. *Mankind*, in *Specimens of the Pre-Shakespearean Drama*, ed. John Matthews Manly (Boston: Ginn, 1897), p. 317.

24. *Cambises*, p. 149.

25. David Wiles, *Shakespeare's Clown* (Cambridge: Cambridge University Press, 1987), p. 21.

26. *Gammer Gurton's Needle*, p. i.

27. *Cambises*, p. 150.

28. In 1574, for example, the boys of Merchant Taylors school were stopped from performing because their behaviour entailed 'such an impudent familiaritie with their betters that often tymes greite contempt of maisters, parents, and magistrats followeth thereof': quoted in Andrew Gurr, *Playgoing in Shakespeare's London* (Cambridge: Cambridge University Press, 1987), p. 129. Thomas Heywood remarks on the widespread assumption that the boys 'juniority' was 'a privilege for any rayling, be it never so violent' (*Apology for Actors*, G3 verso).

29. Ann Thompson, Introduction, *The Taming of the Shrew* (Cambridge: Cambridge University Press, 1984), p. 11.

30. For a description of the sharp fool type, see my *Actor as Anti-Character*, p. 102–7.

31. Coppelia Kahn, *Man's Estate: Masculine Identity in Shakespeare* (Berkeley: University of California Press, 1981), p. 117.

32. See Soule, *Actor as Anti-Character*, p. 162, 167–9.

Scott Magelssen

Accumulation, Loss, and Deferral: Charles Campbell and Steve Epley's Site-Specific Performance 'You Are Here'

This essay is a reflection on the site-specific performance *You are Here*, created by Charles Campbell and Steve Epley on the roof of the University of Minnesota Tate Lab of Physics in May 2002. Scott Magelssen treats the production within the context of the previous site-specific work of Campbell and Epley, and their Minneapolis-based theatre company Skewed Visions, exploring the project's themes of knowledge-production and memory, the company's unique use of space, and the actor-object mode of performance. Scott Magelssen is Assistant Professor of Theatre Arts at Augustana College, Rock Island, Illinois, where he teaches theatre history and dramaturgy, advises the student-run experimental theatre group, and occasionally directs productions. His current research focuses on the performative and historiographic practices employed by outdoor 'living history' museums in Europe and the US.

SQUEEZING out of a cramped and rickety elevator, or winded from climbing several flights of stairs, we have emerged onto the roof of the Tate Lab of Physics, which houses the University of Minnesota's Astronomy Programme. We have gathered here for a performance of *You Are Here*, a site-specific public art project commissioned by the Frederick R. Weisman Museum and sponsored by the Jerome and R. C. Lilly Family Foundations.

Created by Charles Campbell and Steve Epley, *You Are Here* arranges selections of interviews from the occupants of the Astronomy building – graduate students, faculty, administrative and custodial staff – and mingles them with other texts. Campbell, a theatre scholar and practitioner, served as director for the production, whose design and construction – sporting strangely biological/cybernetic contraptions and costume apparatuses – were the responsibility of Epley, a local architectural artist and sculptor. The narrative, Campbell had told me, is framed by an exploration of one individual's pursuit of that which is unattainable or fleeting, and was inspired in part by Jorge Luis Borges' short story *The Aleph*.

Admission to tonight's performance was free, but the size of the audience is limited by the spaces we are to occupy tonight (eventually we will all participate in the climax of the performance in the school's signature observatory dome itself). Hence, the small number of us, about thirty in all, some of whom were individuals interviewed for the piece. The first striking element after we exit onto the roof on this clear, chilly May dusk in Minneapolis, is the jigsaw landscape of the campus below. Normally seen from ground level, or from within its academic halls, the surrounding area appears strange – a network of rooftops, vents, chimneys, and antennae, with the normal buzz of the campus community, muffled and detached, echoing up from below. A familiar environment thus defamiliarized appropriately establishes the mode of witnessing for this evening's performance.

As we shuffle amid the vents, the large satellite dish, and Epley's plywood and metal creations to find unoccupied patches of roof from which we may observe the action to follow, we become aware of the soundscape. The twilight rooftop is set to a regularized percussion of hisses, pulses, and clicks. As Campbell explained to the audience before we ascended to the roof, the sounds have been sampled by sound designers Brett McMullen and Simone Ghetti from noises

The site of the performance from outside: the University of Minnesota's Tate Lab of Physics and observatory dome. Photos for this feature by courtesy of the author.

gathered by large telescopes, actually data in the form of sound, and mixed live during the performance. Not the evocative psychedelic warbling and beeping of a *Dr Who* soundtrack, this is 'space music' which is unfamiliar: mediated and formatted, but not with a familiar aesthetic by which we may recognize and categorize what we hear.

The performance begins as Young Borges (Cherri Macht) appears at the window of a glassed-in overlook. He frantically scribbles chalked equations on the inside of the glass panel (the figures appear backwards to us), intensely chattering over a head mike about the diligence and patience required in gathering information about 'extremely faint objects' with very sensitive instruments over 'unspeakable distances'. Our attention is then directed to Old Borges (Rebecca Myers) seated before us at one of Epley's apparatuses. For Borges' quasi-autobiographical character from *The Aleph* has been split in two: one, the blind old man recalling his days as a young, green academic; the other, that self-same *naif*. Old Borges is fitted with a personal apparatus as

well: a shoulder-mounted rack which perpetually aims two sharp and blinding beams of light into the actor's eyes.

The machine at which Old Borges sits is a desk or work-table of sorts, which intermittently drops ball bearings from a high protrusion mounted on one side. The metal balls strike the inclined surface of the table with a rusty *pang*, then painstakingly roll down the metal trough to the bottom to clack into place with the others in what Beckett may have called an 'impossible heap'.

Young Borges, fitted with a backlit plexiglas writing table jutting from the actor's belly, joins his aged counterpart at the work-table. The two characters take bearings from the pile and sort them into trays. Young Borges pauses to continue scribbling equations with a white grease pencil on his plexiglas.

The ball-bearing image is a visible metaphor of the project's recurrent theme of knowledge-accumulation and production. Like the sounds collected by the telescopes, the data collected by astronomers interviewed by Campbell and Epley are not readily acces-

sible to the naked eye. Rather, as Campbell had explained, the process for accumulating images from deep in space is almost counter-intuitive. It consists of aiming a telescope at a fixed point and gathering information too minute to detect all at once over a long period of time, after which it may be inter-preted with the help of mathematics and astronomical theory.

Of course, Borges' short story features a different kind of knowledge-accumulation. Characters who come into contact with the Aleph behold a shining point in the universe within which all other points are contained and may be seen in an instant – simultane-ously and without overlapping. The absorp-tion of such an all-encompassing, immediate knowledge and truth is a far cry from the work of the University's astronomers, whose unromantic and tedious lot entails the slog-ging collection of raw data over hours or weeks. The image of the gathering of such minutiae and converting them into useable knowledge, however, circulates and rever-berates throughout the performance, playing off the Borges story's themes of memory and the quest for truth.

The onus on the audience, then, is to be engaged in a similar strategy: we are to collect the bits of imagery, sound, dialogue, and experiential navigation through the space and align what we are given into a whole with our own spectatorial apparatus. If the company has a say in what we come away with, the whole may have something to do with the experience of encountering the ordinarily invisible. As the creators state in the programme, the impetus behind the work is to 'manifest in real space' the elements of a place 'that lie outside the visibility of the everyday because of their status as ephem-eral, private, or intangible things.'

At the same time, it is impossible to main-tain the focus and capacity to make a coherent 'whole' out of the multiplicity of images and texts, nor can we glean an overarching mes-sage, conclusion, or moral to this piece. We witness actions, confessions, and shards of a love story, but never long enough for them to coalesce into a grand narrative. Thus, the project carries with it definite feelings of loss and deferral. We learn that there is seldom an ephiphanous arrival at a truth at the end of a prolonged process of searching, owing to the consequences of actions, the inherently fractured quality of memory, or the inescapable limits of knowing.

In astronomy, for every bit of data that is gathered another gap in knowledge emerges, and the 'truths' that are discovered are rarely shocks out of the blue, but anticlimactically postulated only after gruelling calculation and guesswork. Running parallel to this pragmatic exploration, *You Are Here* contains similar themes of loss and anticlimax that emerge in the concurrent narratives. The life of the academic astronomer, for instance, is marked with sacrifices of love and family over career. In *The Aleph,* Borges can never recover his lost Beatriz. Even with the extraordinary and miraculous source of knowledge contained within the Aleph, Borges and other characters are confounded by their own human weaknesses of competition, jealousy, and contempt. The company handles these simultaneous themes with precision as the strands of narrative unfold. Even the climactic moments of the evening substitute teasing collections of imagery and text for a tidy conclusion and denouement.

A Context for 'You Are Here'

Campbell and Epley first collaborated on Skewed Visions Performance Company's *The Eye in the Door Part Three: The Bicycle*, another site-specific performance, in August 1999. In that production, the artists staged an intervention into the normal behaviour patterns of a downtown Minneapolis pedestrian street designed for efficient commerce. At several different 'high-traffic' times of day, two rag-tag tramps (Sarah Corzatt and Rebecca Myers) wended their way down Nicolett Mall with a thirty-foot-long bicycle comprising a sculptural conglomeration of found objects designed by Epley, stopping to enact ritualized scenes.

The Bicycle, Campbell told me, explored notions of urban behaviour control, and, as in *You Are Here*, sought to make visible what was normally hidden from view. In this case, the performance highlighted the tensions created when normal interactions of street-level commerce and transportation were interrupted by elements which have been eliminated from the space (bicycles are not

Opposite: Old Borges (Rebecca Myers), with self-blinding apparatus, seated at ball-bearing machine designed by Steve Epley. Below: Young Borges (Cherri Macht) and Old Borges (Myers) at the ball-bearing machine.

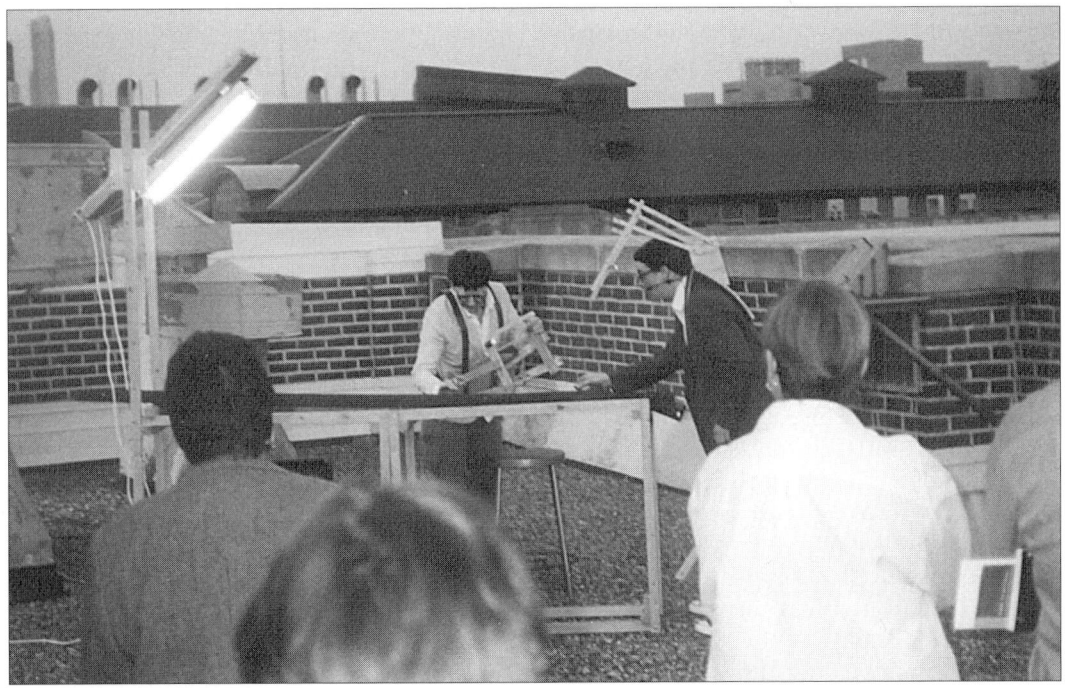

allowed on the Mall, and dirt, riffraff, and litter are cleared twice a day).

The scenes – which included the performers' interaction with several found and manipulated objects (an inside-out clock, a camera), an overturned master-slave relationship, and a duet with an accordion accompaniment – exposed what Campbell called the 'blinders' of the people of Minneapolis. While part of the spectacle was the bicycle and the antics of its riders, an equally fascinating experience for the audience was to watch the ways the businesspeople and the workers either stared at or went out of their way *not* to look at the performance. It had the desired effect, says Campbell. 'These people didn't see it, but others saw them not seeing it.'

The performers' interaction with the bicycle, the exploded clock, etc., furthermore, teased out a theoretical understanding of the relationship between actor and object linked to the work of Polish director Tadeusz Kantor, both Campbell and Epley having recently participated in an extended workshop with Ludmila Ryba, a member of Kantor's company, Cricot 2. Kantor maintained that, after the Second World War, objects on stage may be emptied of their content and endowed with a new identity, as if existing for the first time (Kantor, p. 46). In *The Bicycle*, showing objects which needed interaction with a performer in order to function was a way for the artists to take what was intangible about them – the private, metaphysical, or historical – and bring it out, 'sculpturally'.

Tonight's performance of *You Are Here* features an actor-object mode of performance familiar to Skewed Visions' audiences. Billing itself as 'Minnesota's only site-specific performance company', Skewed Visions was co-founded by Campbell, who now serves as Co-Artistic Managing Director. He holds a PhD in Theatre History and Theory, having written his dissertation on Deleuzian 'nomad art' with reference to practitioners such as Beckett and Kantor. Epley is a provisional company member of Skewed Visions, having recently joined the company along with Cherri Macht. Rebecca Myers is also a member of Skewed Visions, and Nathan Christopher is a veteran of past shows.

Only formed in 1996, Skewed Visions has already established a history of creating visually compelling works of art featuring a sophisticated use and manipulation of public and private space, and engaging with postmodern concepts of the object and the other. Its 1998 *The Eye in the Door Part Two: Breakfast of Champions* took place at the Minneapolis Summer Farmer's Market. Based on the autobiography of an eighteenth-century courtesan, the piece was a satirical commentary on material excess. This became the object of censorship when the performers staged an upper-class feast as a series of *tableaux vivants* which culminated in the orgiastic cannibalization of a woman by the aristocratic guests. The bacchic imagery disturbed shoppers and prompted the market's management to ask that *Breakfast of Champions* be toned down.

Two years later, in a venue with an even more limited audience capacity than for *You Are Here*, Skewed Visions' *The City Itself Part One: The Car* was one of the most talked about selections of the Minneapolis Fringe Theatre Festival in 2000. The spectators consisted of back-seat passengers in a Lincoln Town Car, a taxicab, and an old, beat-up Mazda Protégé. The action took place in the front seats of the cars as they drove through various streets and back alleys of Minneapolis. The backseat spectators were privy not only to the normally invisible interiors of others' vehicles, but also to representations of those situations off the beaten path of civic experience – gunplay and the solicitation of a prostitute, for instance.

The Choice of the Site

You Are Here, while not itself a Skewed Visions production, is no exception to its members' tradition of unpacking what is hidden in private and public arenas. It is the first of three site-specific public art projects commissioned by the Weisman in 2000 for the 2002 Temporary Public Art Program. Campbell and Epley approached the committee with the goal of exposing to a larger public the elements of a university that, though normally outside their experience, are none the less extremely fascinating.

Carlos (Nathan Christopher) and Old Borges (Myers), with apparatuses, deliver simultaneous monologues.

As Campbell told me, the initial university sites considered for the project had to be rejected. Many were too toxic; others (such as the school's controversial steam-heating plant) too politically hot. The ultimate choice was the Astronomy Department – its building physically very visible (Campbell described the observatory dome as the 'symbolic heart of the University'), but its extraordinary practices and knowledge-production experienced only by a handful of individuals.

Over the course of the development of the piece, Campbell and Epley, in the words of the programme, 'conducted interviews with the faculty, students, and staff in the Astronomy Department; did physical evaluation of the spaces; and did [their] own research into current and historical astronomical research, techniques, and instrumentation'. They then gathered the information together for a unique and experiential performance that allowed the audience to encounter these spaces and practices in an aesthetically mediated manifestation.

The resulting performances fell on evenings of special astronomical significance in their own right. Tonight's clear sky holds excellent conditions for stargazing, even in the light-polluted Twin Cities. Just above the horizon this week, the five planets visible from Earth may be clearly seen hovering in close alignment. The next time this happens, I overhear in a conversation next to me as we fasten our coat collars to the neck or stamp in place for warmth, will be sometime in the middle of the twenty-first century.

The Performance Continues

In the opening moments of the performance, the several concomitant narratives begin to emerge out of the collection of texts and visual imagery. Old Borges voices his quest to consecrate himself to his beloved Beatriz's memory, despite her spurning of his advances in life. Young Borges describes how the shape and movement of the galaxies we see from Earth can only make sense if they contain ten times the matter we know about. 'What and where is this DARK MATTER?' Young and Old Borges chant their lines – not a dialogue *per se*, but bits and fragments suggesting the dilemma of expressing that which we cannot see in the universe (black holes, dark matter), interwoven with selections from Borges.

Carlos (Nathan Christopher) now enters and begins to speak simultaneously with the Old and Young Borges. For those who are familiar with the Borges story (or who are able to discern the strain of exposition from the simultaneous dialogue), Carlos is the tiring, overly academic cousin of Beatriz, and, it later emerges, the jealous keeper of the Aleph. Carlos's metaphysical phenomenon, discovered during his childhood and hidden in his basement, supplies him with the information needed for his work in progress: an immense, encyclopedic poem about the earth.

The actors move through the crowd and we follow. Our multi-station journey takes us across the roof from the south deck and around the base of the observatory dome, there to descend into a top-floor classroom space and, finally, to climb up into the observatory. The images arranged by Campbell and Epley for us to encounter are all visually interesting – at times stunning. The characters do not function independently of their machines, which Campbell describes as 'unique amalgams of the practical and suggestive'. Beatriz, a ghost (Juliette Dannucci), enters with a 'wheelcart': a rolling contraption comprised of bobbing and swinging gears and pendula that looks like a Renais-

sance model of the cosmos (and which evokes the title object in Campbell and Epley's last collaboration, *The Bicycle*). A wing-like latex and plywood contraption burdens Carlos's back – bookshelves that fold up into a throne-like chair for the poet.

At one point, we turn the corner to find a box of latex stretched over a wooden frame, onto which a dazzling series of illuminations depicting galaxies, stellar dust, and nebulae is projected. While Old and Young Borges continue their reverie, recalling a visit to Beatriz's family's home to indulge voyeuristically in the framed photographs of the deceased, the silhouette of Beatriz's ghost is seen in the projection box. She presses her face and hands against the latex walls from within, creating a ghoulish relief against the pictures of the universe.

The lines, spoken staccato by the actors, are choppy, stilted fragments rather than smooth streams of input. An unsatisfactory bombardment of syllables and phrases falls on our ears like so many ball bearings ('um

Below: the Ghost of Beatriz (Juliette Dannucci), with wheelcart. Opposite page, top: silhouette of Beatriz (Dannucci) in the latex projection box. Opposite page, bottom right: Young Borges (Macht) with writing-table apparatus. Apparatus in all these photos designed by Epley.

but uh just yeah its too random even if there because it just you start to . . . '). The lines, delivered in two or sometimes three overlapping speeches, are a mix of the interviews, the artists' astronomy research, and Borges' story. Young Borges, for example, telling an anecdote about a first telescope, a father's gift, describes it as not 'one of those cheap crappy things that you know 738 times magnification you know it's like yeah but you can barely see the moon through it um no he actually did a lot of research and he chose you know a good Newtonian telescope'.

Another emergent story suggests the guilty confession of a scholar who elicits joy from taking a notebook and deriving equations in his/her spare time. Someone in the audience laughs. Apparently, she is in on the joke, but the rest of us do not know whether she recognizes the words from her own lips or if she hears the familiar voice of a colleague in the actor's speech.

Not all the site-specific text is wistful and nostalgic, however. As we round the base of the dome where Old Borges is standing alone, he delivers a confession of a different sort. We hear the story of someone who entered academia excited about finding answers to the 'big questions', but gradually, after years of graduate work, found him/herself succumbing to bitterness, feeling jaded and betrayed: 'Because you've been studying physics for so long and you suddenly realize but you can't solve everything you you can't.' More sounds of recognition from the audience. Perhaps other interviewees, mixed with rueful chuckles of those who simply identify with the speaker's disenchantment.

It is these intimate moments, not just the physical use of non-traditional performance space, that really make for the site-specificity of the piece. We are allowed to give ear to the building's denizens, the echoes of whose voices sculpt our movement through space. Here we have another variation on the theme. The material 'accumulated' by the artist-practitioners has been arranged for visual consumption, like the data collected by their subjects. However, by virtue of the nature of performance, the story also belongs to the characters, and informs our perception of them. The anecdotal dovetails with the Borges adaptation to create characters unique to this space and this night.

At the base of the dome, the performance takes an immediate turn as a panicked Carlos, wings spread in a vulture's pose atop a desk/café table, breaks in on the meditative poetry. The owners of his house, Carlos tells Young Borges, are going to have it demolished in order to expand their next-door café. Young Borges panics himself, though in his case it is at the thought of losing the locus of his beloved's memory. Carlos reveals the more intense stakes. His Aleph, discovered as a child by an accident in his cellar, will become forever inaccessible if the demolition plans proceed.

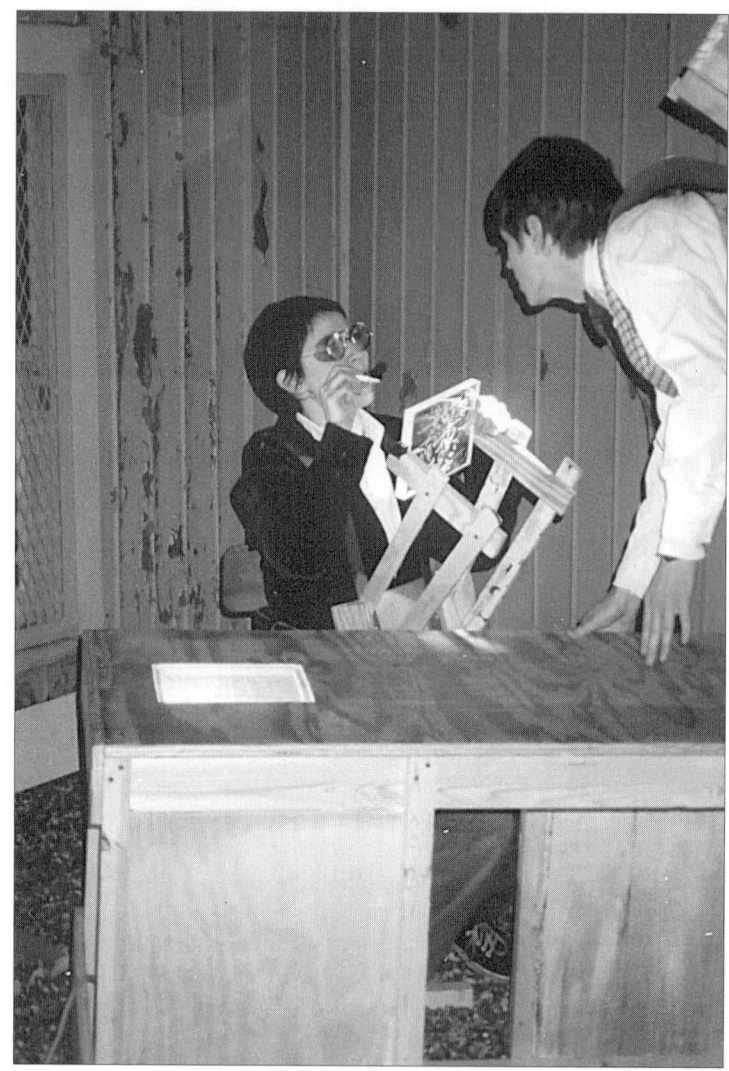

The Aleph and the Binocular Telescope

At this point, the narratives are intertwined and conflated once again, and the political field of the Astronomy Department is made visible in the most intriguing section thus far. Carlos's description of the Aleph is impregnated with references to the 'LBT', the Large Binocular Telescope project currently under way on a mountain in Arizona. As Campbell explained, an international group of institutions, academic and otherwise, 'have come together in a consortium to build a telescope on Mt Graham'. The telescope is aptly named for its two eight-and-a-half-foot diameter mirrors which collect information from deep space using 'adaptive optics' that compen-

Opposite page and above: Young Borges (Macht) and Carlos (Christopher), with apparatuses.

sate for the distortions in the atmosphere ('it can see farther and clearer, with more resolution and more detail . . . than the Hubble Telescope').

In other words, astronomers who are privileged to use the LBT do not actually look through the telescope as Galileo once did, but can access its collected information through a computer from anywhere in the world – a great boon for the University of Minnesota. 'But the mountain itself', continued Campbell, 'is a piece of sacred land to the Apaches in Arizona, and there have been protests in Arizona, there have been protests here.' Not only that, but environmental advocates have also found fault with the LBT project. Its site is the habitat of the Mount Graham Red Squirrel, which is federally listed as an endangered species. When asked by Campbell and Epley about the concerns of the Native Apaches and the environmentalists, the chair of the department answered that the University had understood when coming into the project (after most of the clearing and construction had taken place) that these issues had already been resolved.

If there had been any doubt that the audience would link the description of the Aleph and the references to telescopes and mountains with the LBT project, it was put to rest by the pamphlets handed out by activists in the lobby before the performance. 'Here's some more information', they said, gently but purposefully handing us folded pieces of paper as we made our way to the stairs or elevator. Only after opening the pamphlet did I find it to be a summary of the advocates' arguments for the University to withdraw its participation and funding, and the date and time of a protest rally.

By situating a narrative of the LBT project within the larger narrative of the Aleph story, the production hints at a hubris inherent in the scientific quest for knowledge. The suggestion remains only that, and stops short of weighing in with a political stance (Campbell told me that the group was not interested in political didacticism, as it tends to limit the creative possibilities of theatre).

In the classroom space, though, the subject takes on a cautionary spin. Carlos's lecture on the LBT/Aleph is laced with a simultaneous recital of charged poetry musing on Oedipus (gleaned, I later found from Campbell, from Milan Kundera's *The Unbearable Lightness of Being*). While the King of Thebes did not have knowledge of his own guilt, nevertheless it led to the suffering of the citizens. The situation could only be corrected by Oedipus coming to terms with his own responsibility.

'But enough', Carlos says to us and Young Borges, and beckons us to descend into his cellar to observe the Aleph ('Down with you', he instructs, as he points up into the observatory). We climb the last narrow set of steps into the dome. Once we are packed shoulder-to-shoulder into the tight circumference around the hundred-year-old telescope, we are ready to witness that which has been hinted at in fragments throughout the evening, and the most difficult part of the performance to pull off. Here is where we as an ad hoc community will experience the finish of our shared quest.

Epiphany – or Accumulation?

Campbell and Epley's goal in the beginning was eventually to create an 'epiphany' in the manner of an astronomic discovery taking shape. What the artists arrived at instead became a culmination of the themes of the pursuit of knowledge and the consequent loss and deferral. The climax turns out to be a 'fugue' in three themes, during which Young Borges, Old Borges, and Beatriz hammer an impossible collection of images and descriptions into our consciousness.

The speakers stand against the curved wall in our midst, and each audience member hears a different collage of whispers and chants. A description of a hidden moment in space somewhere on the earth. A reference to the Heisenberg uncertainty principle from somewhere across the room. A bit of familiar text from somewhere else – is it Beckett? Meanwhile, our bearings are hurled into temporary flux as the telescope begins reeling against the walls behind it. The dome is rotating, but in the darkness and alien space we are momentarily uncertain whether we aren't the ones spinning.

Slides are projected from machines situated all around us – flashing images of the familiar and unfamiliar – more quickly than we can take them in. It becomes apparent that we are unable to absorb the bombardment of words, images, and movement: it is only possible at most to focus on a word here, a slide there. Heisenberg's uncertainty principle indeed. As spectators, we are fallible, restricted. Unlike the characters in Borges' story, we are not allowed to witness time and space simultaneously without overlapping.

While the characters are thus privileged, however, we will find they are also prone to human weakness. Following this climax, Carlos interrogates Young Borges. In a petty act of spite, Young Borges will not admit to having witnessed the Aleph. Instead, he recommends that Carlos go to the country to seek rest for his 'condition'. Old Borges shifts to the preterite tense, bringing us back to a mode of remembrance (perhaps, it occurs to me now, we were unable to experience the full scope of the Aleph because we knew it only from the old man's fragmented memory).

Old Borges recalls that the days that followed were terrifying at first. He feared, after having seen everything there was, that nothing would be left to cause surprise. 'Happily', he tells us, 'after a few sleepless nights, forgetfulness began to work in me again.' As Campbell put it to me, the lines signify an irony of Borges' commentary. What began as a search for truth, a consecration to memory, ends in forgetting.

The whole idea of the story is that he's been trying to remember – to retain Beatriz. . . . It's an obsession with him. And then, at the end, he loses Beatriz. But it's in order [for Borges] to go on.

The climax in the dome, if it doesn't convey the sense of epiphany once intended by the creators, is nevertheless a terrifically visceral happening, not to be found in a traditional proscenium theatre. Moments such as this are where site-specificity and community-based performance are immensely provocative and continue to generate new theatrical experience and discussion. Works like *You Are Here* and those of Skewed Visions are especially vital in a place like the Twin Cities.

Despite a strong proliferation of smaller companies here, 'theatre' and 'performance' are synonymous with the Guthrie Theatre on the street. The site-specific work going on in the found spaces of Minneapolis, though, is far more exciting than in its high-profile regional theatre.

New Kinds of Visibility

In its treatment of interview subjects, Borges' short story, and the group's own exploration of the cosmos, *You Are Here* propagates for the spectators a corporally felt knowledge of the specific relationship between actor, spectator, and object. The ball-bearing machine and Young Borges' writing-desk equipage brilliantly convey modes of knowledge-collection in the Astronomy Department, while the apparatus blinding old Borges introduces us to the irony of the selective truth and its dissemination in the quest for clarity and answers. As may be argued, in the postmodern condition the scientific model is predicated on searching for the results only within the realm of that which is already thinkable.

At times, the performance loses its theoretical and aesthetic momentum in the slow pace of some of the delivery. While giving an aural symmetry to the metaphor of data collection, it can nearly bog down the performance, especially outdoors on the roof on a chilly Minnesota spring night. As for the stories of individuals from the Astronomy department, they are nostalgic and quotidian, less profound than Borges' tale but grounding the performance for those to whom it is most important: the community on which the piece is built. All the same, the piece never becomes an uncritical celebration of its subjects. With the looming controversy of the LBT, the characters and interviewees are all complicit in the ramifications of the institutional quest for knowledge. The activists in the lobby drive the indictment home.

Finally, *You Are Here* allows us to share the feelings of loss, deferral, and disappointment endured by the production's characters and interview subjects. These emotions are not transferred by means of a catharsis, but by consistently keeping the epiphany out of reach. The structure of the performance lets us spend time with the characters, but never for long enough to figure them out. Likewise, we are constantly forced to pick the narratives out of the simultaneous strains of spoken texts. We are given too much, by the end, to sort through, and the scrap of a story with which we may or may not emerge comes only after a prolonged strain to gather and filter through the flood of input.

Jean-François Lyotard wrote that, while the function of realism is to soothe the spectator's consciousness from doubt, the postmodern would be that which 'invokes the unpresentable in presentation itself' (Lyotard, p. 15). In attempting to take found spaces outside the quotidian realm and make them visible in new ways, and by experimenting with a multisensory and overwhelming mode of performance, *You Are Here* seeks to fulfil Lyotard's postmodern dictum.

As explained by Campbell, the piece is not meant to translate complex astronomical theory for a lay audience, nor is it meant to give the spectators mechanisms by which to access to or decode universal truths. Rather, a type of knowledge emerges throughout the performance that exists autonomously: truth is a product of subjective selection and organization of enunciations, fragments, information; and loss and forgetting are both the by-products and the requisites of knowledge-production. As Old Borges chants, reflecting the vast unknowable universe, 'What you have is much more than what you see.'

References

Borges, Jorge Luis, *The Aleph and Other Stories 1933–1969*, ed. and trans. Norman Thomas di Giovanni (New York: Dutton, 1970).

Kantor, Tadeusz, *A Journey Through Other Spaces: Essays and Manifestos, 1944–1990*, ed. and trans. Michal Kobialka (Berkeley: University of California Press, 1993).

Lyotard, Jean-François, *The Postmodern Explained*, ed. Julian Pefanis and Morgan Thomas (Minneapolis: University of Minnesota Press, 1992).

Skewed Visions Newsletter, I, No. 1 (Minneapolis: Skewed Visions Performance Company, 2002).

You Are Here programme (Minneapolis: Weisman Art Museum, May 2002).

NTQ Reports and Announcements

DOI: 10.1017/S0266464X04210089

Carl Lavery

Jean Genet: Utopian or Deconstructionist?

Report on the 'Genet in Performance' symposium held at the University of East Anglia on 17–18 October 2003

WHILE Jean Genet's play *Les Bonnes* (*The Maids*) has long been a popular text in British theatres and universities, his more theatrically experimental work, with the possible exception of *Le Balcon* (*The Balcony*), continues to be neglected. It is telling, for instance, that, in spite of the current glut of drama anthologies and performance readers, little is still known in Britain about Genet's radical contribution to the theory and practice of avant-garde theatre. Too often, he is depicted according to the myth – that is to say, as a queer novelist or existential outlaw, and not, as he most certainly is, a key figure in the history of twentieth-century drama.

It was against this background that the 'Genet in Performance' symposium, held at the University of East Anglia's Drama Studio, took place. There were two main intentions: to revise Genet's status in the English-speaking world; and to celebrate the originality and influence of his performance making. The international team of speakers who gathered in Norwich responded to the brief by exploring Genet's experimental work in diverse performance media, including theatre, film, and dance.

In his provocative opening address, entitled 'Theatricality to Performance Theory: the Lesson of Jean Genet', David Bradby, a much respected writer on French theatre, established immediately the tone for the symposium. In the first half of his paper, Bradby argued that the modern discipline of performance studies owes a great debt to Genet's theatrical practice of the 1950s and 1960s that has still to be fully acknowledged. In the second half, he went on to explore the political significance of *Les Paravents* (*The Screens*), Genet's masterpiece about the Algerian war, by describing in detail Patrice Chéreau's production of the play in Paris in 1983 and Peter Sellars's *mise-en-scène* in Los Angeles in 1998. It was difficult to disagree with Bradby's conclusion that in today's mediatized society, Genet's critique of theatricality

has a political dimension that is more relevant than ever.

The first panel on 17 October, 'Theatre as Void: a Graveyard for the Dead', built on Bradby's insights by focusing on the themes of death and the void in Genet's work. Mischa Twitchen began proceedings by explaining how Genet's theatre is a summons to the dead, an attempt to transcend the visible. Carl Lavery went on to politicize that summons by arguing that Genet's aim to awaken the dead is inseparable from a desire to revolutionize everyday life. In Lavery's view, here were clear parallels between Genet's late drama, particularly *The Screens*, and the utopian agenda of the Situationists. Claire Finburgh concluded the panel by explaining how the scenography of *Les Paravents* simultaneously constructs and deconstructs meaning. For Finburgh – and this was a recurrent theme during the symposium – Genet's quest to unveil the void is political. Like Derridean deconstruction, it opens the space for new, always futural, identities to come into being.

The final panel of the day, 'The Vision of Genet: Eye, Camera, and Screen', explored the centrality of the gaze in Genet's aesthetics. In two intriguing presentations, Scott Sherer and Matthew Melia looked at how Genet's articles on Rembrandt and Giacometti in the mid-1950s are not just exercises in art criticism, but sketches for a new theory of theatre. Switching the focus to film, Scott Mackenzie, in a neat deconstruction of Peggy Phelan's argument about the 'ontology of performance', discussed how watching Genet's queer classic, *Un Chant d'amour*, in underground cinemas in the 1960s and 1970s constituted a 'live' performance event in itself.

David Fieni from UCLA brought the day to a close by claiming that the synthetic materials prevalent in Roger Blin's staging of *Les Paravents* in 1966 act as historical and political markers. According to Fieni, the plastic screens used in the production draw attention to the revolution in consumer goods that occurred in 1960s France. At the same time, they comment, ironically and bitterly, on how the Algerian war was treated by the French media. For Fieni, in a memorable phrase, the screens are 'what filter the raw events of the Algerian War – or the real features of the human face – into representable and consumable commodities'.

Events on 18 October began with Albert Dichy, Director of the prestigious IMEC in Paris (Institut Mémoires de l'Édition Contemporaine), defending Genet from the accusations of anti-Semitism made by the French critic and academic Eric Marty in *Bref séjour à Jerusalem* (2003). Although Dichy had little to say about Genet's performance practice, his masterful deconstruction of Marty's argument was intensely relevant to the symposium's overall aim. It proved, beyond any doubt, that, despite the claims of conservative detractors, Genet is a progressive political playwright, whose insights into the Arab world need to be taken seriously, and not dismissed, as they sometimes are, as anti-Semitic.

Dichy's stimulating talk was followed by the most significant panel of the symposium, 'A Historiography of Genet's Drama'. Where the majority of criticism about Genet in performance has been concerned with teasing out its theoretical complexities, relatively little has been written about how his plays have been staged. Deirdre Wilkins, John Warrick, Kara Reilly, and Maria Delgado filled this gap by concentrating on particular productions in specific milieux. Wilkins described Leonor Fini's set designs for J. M. Serreau's production of *Les Bonnes* at the Théâtre de l'Odéon in 1961 and Antoine Bourseiller's staging of *Le Balcon* at the Théâtre du Sud-Est in Marseilles in 1969. Warwick looked at the inflammatory production of *Les Nègres* (*The Blacks*) by Douglas Turner Ward's Negro Ensemble Company at the St Mark's Playhouse in Greenwich Village in 1963. Kara Reilly noted Genet's influence on North American avant-garde theatre by focusing on Herbert Blau's production of *The Balcony* at the Actors' Workshop in San Francisco in 1963. And Maria Delgado explored Victor Garcia's and Nuria Espert's experimental reworking of *Les Bonnes* as *Las Criadas* in Barcelona in 1969.

The success of this panel was due to the way in which the speakers were able to blend historical analysis with performance documentation. Not only was this theoretically innovative, it had a practical dimension too. It showed how Genet's plays, if they are to work successfully in performance, necessitate a rehearsal process that effectively challenges the identities and bodies of the performers.

The body also played an integral part in the next panel of the day, aptly called 'Bodies in/of Performance'. Using Judith Butler's concept of performativity as a methodological tool, Elizabeth Stephens looked at how the dancing body in Genet's ballet *Adame Miroir* and in his film *Un Chant d'amour* is used to construct a theatricalized sense of masculinity for dancer and spectator alike. Paul Woodward tackled the same theme, but from a more autobiographical and confessional perspective. According to Woodward, Genet is a major influence on queer body artists such as Ron Athey and Franko B. because of his celebration of the abject body: the body that pisses, bleeds, and dies. For Woodward, such a celebration, particularly in the age of AIDS, amounts to an act of resistance, a way of valuing experiences and bodies that are conventionally rejected by mainstream society.

The final panel of the symposium, 'Performing Identity in *The Maids*', was given over to practitioners who had grappled with the difficult issue of how best to stage performativity and gender-trouble in the play. Lizzie Eldridge gave an excellent account of her attempts at doing so in her own production of *The Maids* in Edinburgh in 2002 through cross-gender casting and the use of multimedia devices. Parusarum Ramamoorthi told us how he tried to draw attention to the androgynous quality of the text in his Tamil translation of *The Maids*. And finally, Ralph Yarrow, in a practically based paper that had similarities with the work done by Warrick and Delgado, described his techniques for producing a liminal, troubled mind-set for actors rehearsing Genet's plays and the spectators experiencing them.

Appropriately, the symposium was closed by a plenary speech from Michel Corvin, emeritus professor of theatre at Paris III, and editor of *Jean Genet: Théâtre complet* (Gallimard, 2002), a book described by David Bradby as a 'bible for Genet scholars'. Corvin's paper, 'L'humour dans le théâtre de Genet' ('Humour in Genet's Theatre'), synthesized many of the issues raised by other speakers, but did so in a way that was both original and important. Teasing out the hidden meanings of the word 'humour', Corvin argued that it conveys a sense of distance, detachment, and self-consciousness.

In terms of Genet's theatre, this manifests itself in a performance practice which foregrounds its own artificiality, like the dramas of Brecht and Pirandello. Yet, despite the parallels, intimated by Corvin, between Genet, Brecht, and Pirandello, he insisted – and this for me was the point of the paper – that Genet's humour, his practice of meta-theatre, is unique. Where Brecht alienates to instruct and Pirandello to explore metaphysical questions, the intention behind Genet's alienation, argues Corvin, is to combine politics and metaphysics in a 'vertiginous spiral'. Such a tactic transforms fundamentally the very meaning of politics – as no longer about finding answers and offering solutions, but rather becoming a nomadic quest, a process refuting metaphysical notions of beginnings and endings.

As this report hopefully demonstrates, the symposium successfully fulfilled its remit, and showed that Genet's dramatic practice has had a telling influence on contemporary performance art and performance theory. This was reflected in the interest shown in Genet's representation of the body, his concern with issues of performativity and identity, and his anticipation of current trends in performance practice: witnessing, site, hybridization, and use of multimedia devices.

The symposium was also important in that it marked, for instance, a crucial shift in the way Genet's politics are received. Where critics in the 1980s were generally confused about the political significance of his theatre, this is no longer the case. For today's scholars, the crux of the problem lies elsewhere – in whether or not Genet's politics are deconstructionist or utopian. The symposium also heralded, as I mentioned in my discussion of the panel 'A Historiography of Genet's Drama', an exciting new development in Genet studies, one that concentrates not on theory, but on documenting how Genet's plays have been staged by innovative directors and actors.

Given the interest shown in the work of specific practitioners and productions, it was a great pity that Joe Strick, the director of the film version of *The Balcony* (1962), and Barbara Wright, the translator (along with Terry Hands) of the 1972 English edition of the play, were unable to attend because of illness. Their presence was sorely missed. Nevertheless, it did not prevent the symposium from being what I believe it was – an important moment in Genet criticism and for theatre and performance studies in general.

In addition to acknowledging all the delegates for their excellent papers and overall friendliness, I, along with my co-organizer Richard Hibbitt, would like to thank the University of East Anglia Drama Department, Isabelle Joyau, the cultural delegate at the French Institute (L'Institut Français du Royaume Uni) in Cambridge, Granta Books, Screen East, and the British Centre for Literary Translation (BCLT) for their generous sponsorship and help. Thanks are also due to the staff at the UEA Drama Studio, and the French-language theatre company, Sacré Théâtre, based at UEA, who had the unenviable task of performing *Les Bonnes* in front of an audience of informed critics.

DOI: 10.1017/S0266464X04220085

Month-Long Birthday Party for Odin Teatret

Plans for the celebration of Odin's fortieth birthday, September–October 2004

ODIN TEATRET will celebrate its fortieth birthday in October 2004 with a wealth of activities in Holstebro and Aarhus.

The main events will be two international symposia. The first, in collaboration with the University of Aarhus, is entitled *Why a Theatre Laboratory?*

and will take place from 4 to 6 October. It will discuss the concept of the 'theatre laboratory'. What do we mean by this? Which groups or institutions may be so categorized? Do objective criteria exist for defining a 'laboratorial' identity? What does the work of Stanislavsky and Decroux, Meyerhold and Peter Brook, Grotowski and Mnouchkine, Copeau and Odin Teatret have in common?

These questions will be taken up by leading specialists in the field – Georges Banu, Eugenio Barba, Raquel Carrió, Exe Christoffersen, Marco De Marinis, Leszek Kolankiewicz, Patrice Pavis, Zbigniew Osinski, Béatrice Picon-Vallin, Janne Risum, Franco Ruffini, Nicola Savarese, Richard Schechner, Mirella Schinom and Ferdinando Taviani. A living legacy will be present through demonstrations by Gennadi Bogdanov (Meyerhold), Théâtre du Mouvement (Decroux), and Odin Teatret.

The second international symposium, *The Theatre that Dances* from 7 to 10 October, also in Aarhus, deals with the aspects of a theatre whose sensorial and dynamic characteristics have become a genre in itself. There will be practical sessions, lectures, working demonstrations, and performances by the following theatres: The Song of the Goat, Poland; Théâtre du Mouvement, France; Augusto Omolú, Brazil; Granhoej Dans and Odin Teatret, Denmark.

The many other activities celebrating Odin Teatret's fortieth birthday will begin in mid-September and end in mid-October. Among them will be a seminar at the CTLS (Centre for Theatre Laboratory Studies) at the University of Aarhus, about *Professional Identity and Interculturalism*, dealing with the influence of Peking Opera in Europe and of western texts and performing styles on the Peking opera. In Holstebro, Odin Teatret's base since 1966, there will also be a closed symposium about *The Local Roots and Distant Contacts of a Theatre Laboratory*, several guest performances, and a three-week theatre project for children in collaboration with the Brazilian theatre Udi Grudi.

Sixty international participants will be selected for the symposia in Aarhus.

WHY A THEATRE LABORATORY?
4–6 October 2004. *Fee:* DKK 750.

THE THEATRE THAT DANCES
7–10 October 2004. *Fee:* DKK 1000.

For application forms and detailed information about the many events, see www.odinteatret.dk

NTQ Book Reviews

edited by Bella Merlin

DOI: 10.1017/S0266464X04210090

Clare McManus
Women on the Renaissance Stage:
Anna of Denmark and Female Masquing
in the Stuart Court 1590–1619
Manchester: Manchester University Press, 2002.
276 p. £45.00 (hbk); £14.99 (pbk).
ISBN: 0-7190-6092-3 (hbk), 0-7190-6250-0 (pbk).

In his account of the performance of the masque *Hymenaei* Ben Jonson famously drew a distinction between his published text and a performative 'text' which could not be captured in print: 'So short lived are the bodies of all things in comparison with their souls'. In contradiction to Jonson's formulation and to scholarly tradition, Clare McManus's deft and scholarly study forces its reader to pay equal attention to the 'body' of the masque, its impact in performance, and the complex cultural and political networks which led to its manifestation in the early Jacobean court.

Approaching Jacobean female performance as a 'phenomenon in its own right', Clare McManus focuses on the activities of its foremost patron, Queen Anna of Denmark, tracing her masquing career through the early experiments of *The Vision of the Twelve Goddesses* and *The Masque of Blackness* to the innovatory inclusion of a female voice in Robert White's *Cupid's Banishment*, performed in 1617. Although it might look like a simple substitution of royal authority for that of the dramatist or the architect, the decision to use Anna herself as the centre of discussion is a significant one. It allows McManus to draw in a wide range of valuable texts and contexts, which include Anna's upbringing in the Danish court, the entertainments staged in Edinburgh and Stirling prior to her husband's accession to the English throne, her political roles before and after 1603, and her patronage of neglected masque texts, notably *Cupid's Banishment* and Thomas Campion's *Somerset Masque*.

Certain themes recur: the relationships between female vocality and silence, language and sexuality, and gender and class. McManus provides detailed discussions of the effect of the juxtaposition of elite female masquers and professional male actors, and the intersection between staging, costume, and the performing female body; her emphasis on the central importance of dance to the genre is particularly welcome. She demonstrates that the structures and conventions of courtly behaviour enabled elite female performance, although the physical presence of the aristocratic female body could simultaneously disrupt courtly hierarchies.

Anna's dramatic 'canon' is fairly small, but its impact can be traced in the dramatic activities of Henrietta Maria, her successor as queen consort, and in the eventual introduction of professional female actors at the Restoration. This important book should inspire further investigation of the cultural activities of Jacobean women and of the wider traditions in which they operated.

LUCY MUNRO

DOI: 10.1017/S0266464X04220097

Lukas Erne
Shakespeare as a Literary Dramatist
Cambridge: Cambridge University Press, 2003.
300 p. £45.00.
ISBN: 0-521-82255-6 (hbk).

Lukas Erne's superb book is a hardbacked monograph, an expensive publication that is targeted towards specialists in the field of early modern drama. However, its conclusions are so engaging that its arguments will become well known by a generation or more of Shakespeareans. The basic point of the book is quite straightforward: published versions of Shakespeare's plays are not derisory, careless souvenirs of theatrical performances. In fact, Shakespeare and his company took pains to prepare texts that they knew would be read with care, interest, and precision.

For Erne, there are two types of printed Renaissance play. One type of book represents a play's 'theatrical' presentation, while the other type conveys a 'reading' version of the play. To support his argument, Erne shows us that early modern play texts were printed and sold in great numbers; that, in collaboration with the bookselling trade, playing companies such as Shakespeare's orchestrated and timed their publications; and that increasingly literate consumers catalogued, read, and studied them with reflective seriousness.

Shakespeare, already a major literary name by the late 1590s, was marketable in the bookshops as well as in the theatres. His printed dramas were read as closely as his printed narrative poems. Erne argues that the first, short Quarto of *Hamlet* tells us how Shakespeare's company acted the play. The second, long Quarto of the play gives us a 'literary' *Hamlet* that Shakespeare wanted us to read and reflect upon. Scholars have disagreed for decades about the means of textual transmission that led to the publication of so-called 'bad'

Quartos such as the 1603 *Hamlet*. Erne dismisses theories that they showcase actors' faulty memories of plays or that they are 'regional' versions presented in tours outside London. Indeed, Erne rejects the judgemental notion that these texts are 'bad' at all. They are, fundamentally, just generically distinct from their 'reading' versions.

He goes on to insist that Shakespeare's full version of *Hamlet*, published in 1604, would not have been acted in the playhouse, but that this 'reading' version is not more or less authentically Shakespearean than the short version published a year before. Both are equally valid, but their appeal is of two different kinds: shorter, less wordy 'acting' versions of the plays work to animate our senses; while the less visceral 'reading' editions are designed to appeal to our intellect.

Erne is respectful towards performance criticism, but critical of its limitations. He suggests that the drive to edit and critique Shakespeare's plays as they were 'originally performed' misses the point that the extant texts were sometimes contrived to work on the page rather than in the theatre. Erne concludes with a rousing call to return to some sort of character criticism, one that would – for example – note that Old Capulet is a more nuanced and rounder character in the long, 'reading' version of *Romeo and Juliet* than he is in the short, 'acting' version of the play.

Erne's book is marvellously researched, meticulously annotated, sensitively illustrated, and delivered in clear, refulgent prose. Not everyone will agree that the troubling existence of 'good' and 'bad' Shakespearean play texts can be so easily explained, but every reader will be stimulated and provoked.

KEVIN DE ORNELLAS

DOI: 10.1017/S0266464X04230093

Simon Goldhill

Who Needs Greek? Contests in the Cultural History of Hellenism
Cambridge: Cambridge University Press, 2002.
326 p. £15.95.
ISBN: 0-521-01176-0.

Only the central chapter of the five that comprise the substance of this fascinating and illuminating study is directly concerned with theatre, drama, and performance. However, anyone interested in reception studies should read this account of moments in cultural history when concepts, hermeneutics, and ideals linked to ancient Greece and its language have become of passionate and intellectual ideological contemporary concern. As Goldhill argues, '"Reception" is too blunt, too *passive* a term for the dynamics of resistance and appropriation, recognition, and self-aggrandisement that make up this drama of cultural identity.'

Chapter 3 ('Blood from the Shadows: Strauss's Disgusting Degenerate *Elektra*') gives a detailed and nuanced account of the context and conflicts surrounding both the first English performance in 1910 and the original performance in Berlin in 1903 of Strauss's and Hofmannsthal's recreation of the Sophoclean text. The analysis shows not only how a contemporary creative reworking of an ancient tragedy can become 'the expression of a crisis in cultural identity, but also how this crisis takes on different – and *interactive* – forms in Germany and England'. Chapters on Erasmus and the conflict surrounding the promulgation of the Greek language, the notion of 'being' Greek as negotiated in the works of Lucian, early and late nineteenth-century appropriations of the Greek in English culture, education, and society, and the changing attitudes to the value and importance of Plutarch in recent history complete this study of some exemplary 'critical moments when cultural identity has become inextricably linked with an idea of Greek and Greek becomes a bitterly contested area of social and intellectual activity'.

L. DU S. READ

DOI: 10.1017/S0266464X0424009X

Katherine Bliss Eaton, ed.

Enemies of the People
Evanston, Illinois: Northwestern University Press, 2002. 230 p. $79.95.
ISBN: 0-8101-1769-X.

This book brings out more tragedies of Russian intellectuals and artists in the Stalinist years. It is not wholly focused on theatre: its eleven essays by different contributors also cover poetry, film, the novel, and satirical writing. This suggests that the book is somewhat arbitrary in its choice of subject, though in that perhaps it reflects Stalin's own attitude. Dictatorship is always more potent when no one knows who the next victim will be. There are some inaccuracies, which may worry the reader. For instance, it has been known for ten years that Sergei Tretyakov was not shot, but threw himself over the banisters at Butryki Prison (the authorities put nets across the stairwell after that to ensure that no one could follow his example).

Essays on Isaac Babel and the two on women poets (especially that by Diana Lewis Burgin on the brilliant lesbian poet, Sophia Parnak) are of particular interest. Babel's plays certainly deserve more attention than they have ever received in Britain. Edward Braun's meticulous and moving account of the last months in the life of Vsevelod Meyerhold (which was first published in the pages of this journal) retains its awful power and is properly preserved in this book.

Lynn Malley provides an exemplary and thought-provoking account of the rise and fall of TRAM, the theatre of Leningrad working-class youth, which spawned a number of descendant TRAMS and flourished in the period of the first Five-Year Plan, before being gobbled up by the ubiquitous dictatorship. Also noteworthy is Jeffrey Veidlinger's discussion of the Jewish theatres of the time, which provided the kind of fare which enabled Jewish audiences to see beyond the cruel banalities to which they were subject to a kind of utopian subtext which they shared with the performers. It may be argued that one great value of the oppressive weight of the Soviet machine on the theatre was that it helped to develop a unique kind of spectator who was, at least partly, capable of what Brecht called 'complex seeing'.

ROBERT LEACH

DOI: 10.1017/S0266464X04250096

Aleks Sierz
In-Yer-Face Theatre: British Drama Today
London: Faber, 2003. 274 p. £9.99.
ISBN: 0-571-20049-4.

First published in 2001, *In-Yer-Face Theatre* is a pithy encapsulation and bold analysis of a new aesthetic of theatre trends which erupted in 1990s Britain, a decade wherein, in Sierz's words, 'Never before had so many plays been so blatant, so aggressive or emotionally dark.' Sierz's introduction and first chapter ('What Is In-Yer-Face Theatre?') are clear and articulate in their mission and remit: this is an essentially personal and deliberately polemical assessment of British theatre, placing the playwright right at the centre of the theatrical experience. That said, the visceral transaction between stage and audience is also of vital importance.

The style of the book is exciting and accessible, with chapters devoted to Anthony Neilson, Sarah Kane, and Mark Ravenhill, while a host of other writers – including Phyllis Nagy, Jez Butterworth, Patrick Marber, and Judy Upton – are featured in other sections focusing on 'Boy' plays, 'Sex Wars', and plays of violence. Although the playwright remains at the centre of Sierz's study, inevitably attention is granted to particular theatres which promoted new writing – including the Royal Court, the Bush, and Birmingham Rep – as well as pioneering theatre companies and directors, one of the most significant being Max Stafford-Clark and his Out of Joint company. (It was Stafford-Clark who propelled Ravenhill's *Shopping and Fucking* from fringe status to the mainstream West End.)

What emerges with vivacity and force from Sierz's compelling book is that 'in-yer-face' theatre (the term derives from American sports journalism of the 1970s, implying 'that you are forced to see something close up, that your personal space has been invaded') has five vital components. It is a theatre of sensation; it uses shock tactics; it questions moral norms; it is experiential, not speculative; and it tells us more about who we

are. In other words, 'in-yer-face' theatre was a reflection of British society at the end of the millennium, and one of its key 'shock tactics' was the predominant use of intimate performance venues. The actual physical space in which an audience found itself confronted with the images of its own society was an important means by which the theatre could exercise its politics.

There is a journalistic style to Sierz's book which in many ways both embraces and reflects the ideas and dramatic strategies of which he is writing. It also renders the book extremely accessible to the student reader seeking a vivid and provocative introduction to late twentieth-century British theatre, as well as to the social scientist intrigued by the anatomy of a culture. I have no doubt that *In-Yer-Face Theatre* will form a kind of textbook for contemporary theatre courses: the fact that it has been reprinted within two years manifestly illustrates its use and readability.

BELLA MERLIN

DOI: 10.1017/S0266464X04260092

Anthony Kubiak
Agitated States: Performance in the American Theater of Cruelty
Ann Arbor: University of Michigan Press, 2002. 239 p. £39.00 (hbk), £18.00 (pbk).
ISBN: 0-472-09811-x (hbk), 0-472-06811-3 (pbk).

This is an intellectually ambitious text, which reads American history as theatre, and theatre as an enactment of American historical blindness. Using the psychoanalytical theory of Lacan as a backdrop, Kubiak produces a nuanced reading of American texts and contexts, and moves across different levels and aspects of performance (if not performativity) in his critique. His stance is anti-cultural materialist and anti-critical theory, but this is no reactionary diatribe. Rather, he produces a critique of positions that may be blind to the very theatricality which they seem to be critiquing.

Incidents in American history which are read through theatre and psychoanalysis include the assassination of President Lincoln, the events of 9/11, the Columbine High School murders, the rise of dissociative identity disorder and claims of (ritual) sexual abuse, the trials of O. J. Simpson and Timothy McVeigh, and various religious movements which involve a sort of out-of-body (and theatricalized) performance.

Kubiak provides detailed analysis of a range of plays, beginning with Royall Tyler's *The Contrast* (1787) and Anna Cora Mowatt Ritchie's *Fashion* (1845). Other plays addressed at length include Joseph Jefferson's *Rip Van Winkle*, Dion Boucicault's *The Octoroon*, Eugene O'Neill's *Desire under the Elms*, Edward Albee's *Who's Afraid of Virginia Woolf?*, and Sam Shepard's *Buried Child*. He also reads non-dramatic literature, including a Hawthorne short story, Puritan diaries, and *Moby Dick*, as well as performance theatre from minstrelsy to the work of Beatrice Roth and Karen Finley. He finishes with a discussion of Tony Kushner's *Angels in America* and Suzan-Lori Parks's *America Play*.

Kubiak insists that America is an inherently theatrical culture, and explores its history through texts and events that recapitulate moments of aphasia, amnesia, blindness, hysteria, and grief. The writing is clear, convincing, and acute; this book will make an important addition to any American theatre (or even cultural history) course.

HEIDI SLETTEDAHL MACPHERSON

DOI: 10.1017/S0266464X04270099

S. E. Wilmer
Theatre, Society, and the Nation: Staging American Identities
Cambridge: Cambridge University Press, 2002. 281 p. £45.00.
ISBN: 0-521-80264-4.

This useful and impressive book examines how theatre and other forms of performance have influenced the articulation and production of cultural identities in the United States from the second half of the eighteenth century to the present. Following an introduction that offers some critical and international context as well as an overview of the book, seven chronologically ordered chapters focus on case studies of significant performance in transitional eras in American history: Federalist and Democratic theatre before independence; native religious ritual and/of resistance in the late nineteenth century; workers' pageants in the early twentieth century; Black, Chicano/a and anti-war theatre in the 1960s; suffragette and feminist theatre in the early and mid-late twentieth century; and mixed-race theatre and performance art practices of the 1990s.

While Wilmer provides examples of patriotic performance, he argues for a more nuanced understanding of that which may at first appear simply patriotic, and he focuses on performance that he describes as being counter-hegemonic. He grounds close readings of plays and performances in extensive historical and cultural context, and rigorously examines plays' performance, reception, and impact as well as their literary form, content, and rhetoric. The book does not aim to be comprehensive, but provides a useful indicative history, surveying not only significant moments in American cultural history but also an important range of issues (related to, for example, political affiliation, race, class, and gender), as well as a diverse range of performance practices (including plays, ritual, pageantry, and performance art).

The book is both fluent and scholarly, combining lucid and detailed description with committed ideological engagement and analysis, as well as providing a solid academic apparatus of notes, bibliography, and index. It is a welcome contribution to the study of American theatre and culture more broadly, and, comparatively, other national cultures and their performance practices.

JEN HARVIE

DOI: 10.1017/S0266464X04280095

Richard Boon
About Hare: the Playwright and his Work
London: Faber, 2003. 241 p. £8.99.
ISBN: 0-571-21429-0.

David Hare is the playwright whom it is fashionable for academics and students to love to hate. It is rare to hear a conversation about the state of British new writing without someone passing a jibe against this New Labour knight. Like Terence Rattigan before him, Hare carries on his shoulders a number of accumulated frustrations, irritations, and anxieties of theatre professionals – especially those interested in cutting-edge drama.

In some ways, it is not difficult to see why: Hare's journey from the left-wing radical who co-founded the fringe Portable Theatre group to mainstream kingpin with a string of West End hits prompts accusations of 'selling out'. Plays such as *Amy's View* (1997) and *The Breath of Life* (2002), with their appeal to middlebrow, middle-class audiences, may suggest cultural complacency. Added to this, his own uninhibited voicing of opinions in the press have not always endeared him to those who disagree either with his politics or his theatrical vision. And yet, as this superb new book by Richard Boon makes clear, most of what David Hare has to say about theatre is not only correct but also deeply and pertinently revealing of British culture in general.

Boon's introduction neatly charts the playwright's career and offers a simple introduction to British post-war economics, society, and politics – Hare's characteristic theme. He shows how Hare evolved from being a political writer into a moral playwright. He goes on to give a clear and sympathetic account of his work, which has appeared on all kinds of stages (from fringe touring venues to the National Theatre), as well as on television and film. His account of the collaborative classic, *Fanshen* (1975) is typically lucid.

But the hallmark of this new Faber series is a focus on what the playwrights have to say about their own work; and Boon has expertly put together extracts from Hare's interviews and essays, and then added a selection of new interviews with actors such as Bill Nighy and Lia Williams (who starred in *Skylight* in 1995), and theatre-makers such as designer Vicki Mortimer and director Richard Eyre. Apart from occasional quibbles (Boon's analysis of *Skylight* highlights the politics of the main characters, but ignores the emotional core of the work, Tom's betrayal of Kyra's trust), this readable, concise, and detailed book is an excellent introduction to Hare's work.

ALEKS SIERZ

DOI: 10.1017/S0266464X04290091

Michael Mangan
Staging Masculinities
Palgrave, Macmillan, 2003. 288 p. $24.95.
ISBN: 0-333-72019-9.

This book (as the author himself remarks) is one of a growing number of texts that deal explicitly with an area of gender and performance studies that has, until recently, been something of a blank. A vast amount of work has been done teasing out the various meanings that have attached themselves to women in performance history; but until relatively recently the other half of the equation – the figure of the man – has been left comparatively unexplored, men tending to be regarded as the inflexible norm against which the problematic status of women can be measured.

It could be argued that this was a necessary strategy (after all, women had been treated as the unstable other in gender relations for centuries; feminist theorists converted that apparent weakness into a source of strength). However, the argument does cut both ways: if the figure of the woman shifts through history, then, almost by definition, the figure of the man must do so too. The genders are culturally intertwined in a complex relation of similarity and difference; and this particular cultural moment, one in which (by all accounts) masculinity is in crisis, would seem an apt time to reconsider the mutations in the apparently fixed and stable image of men.

It is to Mangan's credit that he refuses to see masculinity as a fixed category that has come under recent attack. Rather, he argues that masculinity has always been in crisis – the male self-image, as revealed in performance, always curiously unfixed – but that the crisis itself does not stay the same. Drawing on a comprehensive range of texts (from liturgical drama to *Oleanna* and *Defending the Caveman*), Mangan traces the complex relation between the presentation of men on stage and the social role that maleness occupies in the society surrounding the performance.

Some of the arguments are familiar (the presence of the boy actors serves to destabilize gender roles); some are rather less so (Mangan is particularly good on the sheer complexity of male roles on the eighteenth- and nineteenth-century stages). Taken together, the case studies do amount to an impressively detailed and persuasive case: that gender relations have always been unfixed, and representations of maleness cannot be divorced from then-contemporary ideas of gender, irrespective of the historical period under discussion.

Too many texts concerned with the area deal either with a theoretically abstracted, entirely contemporary or narrowly contextualized model of gender relations. It is good to read a text that concisely and effectively presents a wider picture. This will be a useful text for undergraduates studying the relation of gender to performance: it should also prove useful to anyone interested in the social context of performance.

DAVID PATTIE

DOI: 10.1017/S0266464X04300096

James Fisher
The Theater of Tony Kushner: Living Past Hope
New York; London: Routledge, 2001. 288 p. $19.95.
ISBN 0-415-94271-3.

Kushner's reputation rests on his artistic and commercial success in the 1990s with *Angels in America*. But as James Fisher is at pains to demonstrate in this study, his achievement in *Angels* has tended to overshadow his other work, which includes his provocative if not entirely successful earlier full-length plays *A Bright Room Called Day* and *Hydriotaphia, or The Death of Dr Browne*, his post-*Angels* tragicomic meditation on the fall of Communism in *Slavs!*, and a fair number of adaptations and one-act pieces. While he devotes a substantial chapter to *Angels in America*, the virtue of Fisher's book is that he offers a comprehensive analysis of this other work, including details of productions and surveys of critical response; and it is this thoroughness rather than anything particularly novel or illuminating in Fisher's approach that will make the book a useful accompaniment to any serious study of Kushner's work.

The 'Introduction' stresses Kushner's socialism and his Brechtian inspiration, as well as his relationship to American gay culture and playwriting. The playwright has himself noted the oddness of calling oneself a socialist in contemporary America; but for all the emphasis on it in this book – and despite Kushner's evidently helpfully co-operative relationship with its author – one discovers disappointingly little beyond a few rather sonorous platitudes about the nature or implications of the dramatist's political commitment. Nor does Fisher devote enough attention to Kushner's artistic relationship with Brecht – the ways in which a contemporary, left-wing, gay American playwright must interrogate and perhaps reject his model as well as be inspired by it.

One can't help feeling that more justice would have been done to this most thought-provoking of contemporary dramatists if Fisher had allowed himself to be less intent on comprehensiveness and rather less blandly reverential in attitude, and more prepared to broach the critical issues raised by Tony Kushner's theatre at its most exciting.

BRIAN CROW

DOI: 10.1017/S0266464X04310092

Elinor Fuchs and Una Chaudhuri, ed.
Land/Scape/Theater
Ann Arbor: University of Michigan Press, 2002.
390 p. £42.50 (hbk), £21.50 (pbk).
ISBN: 0-472-09720-2 (hbk), 0-472-06720-6 (pbk).

This book examines the paradigm of landscape as a model for the way in which theatre and performance engage with our sense of space and place. Sixteen essays expand the paradigm to embrace a wide variety of historical and contemporary performance practice. Landscape began as a device for 'picturing' the world and its spaces, and as such it is intrinsically a theatrical construct: it is the staging of a cultural fiction. It rapidly became central to the aesthetic and the dramaturgy of the nineteenth century. At its close the avalanches of Ibsen, the threatened forests of Chekhov, and the landscape of the *Festspielhaus* in Bayreuth provide the scenography and the architecture of twentieth-century theatre.

Elinor Fuchs pursues this in a lucid analysis of the American myth of the land, of Willy Loman's 'conflicted landscape', of the urban built environment and the pastoral nostalgia of the disappearing open space. In the theatre of Sam Shepard and Suzan-Lori Parks and in the performance of David Hancock, landscape dramaturgy provides a 'primary lens' through which to comprehend human culture. Natalie Crohn Schmitt explores the centrality of real landscape in the plays of Yeats, and Joseph Roach subverts the traditional scenography of *Waiting for Godot* by locating the play in the landscape of the Irish potato famine, where 'the cold-blooded modernity of the Great Hunger foreshadows an apocalyptic global landscape yet to come'. 'Sweet mother earth!' says Estragon.

Stanton B. Garner Jr. considers the urban space and looks at ways in which it may become the landscape of contemporary performance art, in which scenographic practice and environmental theatre find ways of incorporating the material context of performance into the theatrical event itself. Pursuing Gertrude Stein's consideration that dramaturgy might exist in and for itself, like a painted landscape, Marc Robinson writes on the ways in which Nicholas Poussin sought and Robert Wilson seeks the essential structures of individuals – forms beneath personality, of a difference between seeing and looking – in his analysis of Wilson's *Lohengrin*.

Stein's *langscapes* are refined and extended in Marvin Carlson's study of Richard Foreman and Eric Overmeyer. Essays by Edward Ziter and Charlotte Canning take us back to staging the exotic in nineteenth-century imperial melodrama, and the locus of the touring Chautauqua tent in American culture, and yet expand still further the paradigm of landscape. Both provide a thought-provoking preface to Julie Stone Peter's account of Artaud's atavistic search for an ideal theatre in the Tarahumara landscapes of the Sierra Madre.

This accumulative resonance is enhanced as Matthew Wilson Smith considers the total landscaping of Wagner's Bayreuth *Festspielhaus* alongside the contemporary *Gesamtkunstwerk* of 'main street USA' at Disneyland. Alice Raynor's study of virtual landscapes of cyberspace concludes the book. In sum, this is a stimulating and original collection of essays that transforms and grows with each new essay – a quite remarkable product of thought, and committed and inventive editing.

CHRISTOPHER BAUGH

DOI: 10.1017/S0266464X04320099

Elizabeth Klaver
Performing Television: Contemporary Drama and the Media Culture
USA: University of Wisconsin Press, 2000.
145 p. £19.95.
ISBN: 0-87972-826-4.

Elizabeth Klaver focuses on theatre pieces that 'perform' television by using its structures and discourses reflexively to critique its place in 'the mediated Imaginary' (her term is indicative of her enthusiasm for Jacques Lacan and the post-Lacanians). She argues that 'all discussion by drama about television is ultimately a self-reflexive discussion and pertains, in particular, to the issue of subjectivity and identity of postmodern drama and theatre in a media culture'. This quotation typifies not only a clogged style but also a persistent conflation throughout the book of 'drama' and 'theatre' (and 'drama and theatre' are 'genres', according to the flyleaf). She appears not to recognize a distinct category of 'television drama' and to have little appetite for television at all.

Alert in an almost genuflecting way to the nuances of her post-structuralist mentors, Klaver is resolutely vague about actually-existing conditions of performance and reception – even in the USA, whence come most of her examples. Theatrical productions and television shows alike remain indeterminately 'out there'. There are over-generalized, totalizing initial questions like, 'Is theatre a viable art form given the overpowering presence of television?' and a conclusion that asserts that 'Theatre is not in competition with television and can only benefit from recognizing shared interests and a shared place.'

Klaver's theatrical examples include ingenious purveyors of television structures and images (The Wooster Group, Megan Terry, Luis Valdez) and she has a useful section on the 1990 *Beckett Directs Beckett* US TV series. For me, the best chapter was her third, in which extended analysis of the 'mediated Imaginary' is thought-provoking.

DEREK PAGET